PRAISE FOR SMALL MERCIES

Winner of The Viacom Canada Writers' Trust Non-Fiction Award

"This remembrance—a precisely detailed miniature—appears to the reader to be so direct and immediate as to be almost effortless ... This memoir does more than recall a past. It reclaims it, and with no device other than unerringly beautiful writing."—*Sandra Gwyn, David Macfarlane, and Ronald Wright, Viacom Canada Writers' Trust Non-Fiction Award jury citation*

"Hillen describes, vividly and with astonishing recall, his life in a new country in a coming-of-age memoir laced with familiar ingredients: feelings of emotional and geographic displacement, adolescent angst, sexual uncertainty, and the uncertainty, too, of an uncharted future." —*The London Free Press*

"*Small Mercies* is a book of small pleasures; after the horrors of war, Hillen revels in the quotidian victory of being alive. Small wonder." —*Saturday Night*

"What makes *Small Mercies* interesting is not so much Hillen's personality as his character, which illuminates these pages with something like an inner glow ... There ought to be a place for this style of gentle reminiscence on all bookshelves. Underneath the book's gentle ebb and flow, there is a tough edge. Being true to yourself, Ernest Hillen contends, is an end-game worth winning—and that's what makes his book worth reading."—Peter C. Newman, *The Globe and Mail*

PENGUIN CANADA

SMALL MERCIES

ERNEST HILLEN was born in Holland and moved to Indonesia when he was three. During the Second World War, he spent three and half years in Japanese prison camps in Java. He immigrated to Canada in 1952, where he has written for and edited a variety of Canadian magazines, including *Maclean's*, *Weekend Magazine*, and *Saturday Night*. He is also the author of *The Way of a Boy: A Memoir of Java*.

Bayfield, Ont.
June, '08

SMALL
A BOY AFTER WAR
MERCIES

To Mary:
Thank you for the
Festival!

Ernest Hillen

Ernest Hillen

PENGUIN
CANADA

PENGUIN CANADA

Published by the Penguin Group

Penguin Group (Canada), 90 Eglinton Avenue East, Suite 700, Toronto, Ontario,
Canada M4P 2Y3 (a division of Pearson Canada Inc.)

Penguin Group (USA) Inc., 375 Hudson Street, New York, New York 10014, U.S.A.
Penguin Books Ltd, 80 Strand, London WC2R 0RL, England
Penguin Ireland, 25 St Stephen's Green, Dublin 2, Ireland
(a division of Penguin Books Ltd)
Penguin Group (Australia), 250 Camberwell Road, Camberwell, Victoria 3124, Australia
(a division of Pearson Australia Group Pty Ltd)
Penguin Books India Pvt Ltd, 11 Community Centre, Panchsheel Park,
New Delhi – 110 017, India
Penguin Group (NZ), 67 Apollo Drive, Rosedale, North Shore 0632, New Zealand
(a division of Pearson New Zealand Ltd)
Penguin Books (South Africa) (Pty) Ltd, 24 Sturdee Avenue, Rosebank,
Johannesburg 2196, South Africa

Penguin Books Ltd, Registered Offices: 80 Strand, London WC2R 0RL, England

First published in a Viking Canada hardcover by Penguin Group (Canada),
a division of Pearson Canada Inc., 1997
Published in Penguin Canada paperback by Penguin Group (Canada),
a division of Pearson Canada Inc., 1998
Published in this edition, 2008

1 2 3 4 5 6 7 8 9 10   (WEB)

Copyright © Ernest Hillen, 1997
Introduction copyright © Charlotte Gray, 2008

Some of the names have been changed for reasons of privacy.

Manufactured in Canada.

Library and Archives Canada Cataloguing in Publication data available upon
request to the publisher.

ISBN: 978-0-14-316852-2

Visit the Penguin Group (Canada) website at **www.penguin.ca**

Special and corporate bulk purchase rates available; please see **www.penguin.ca/
corporatesales** or call 1-800-810-3104, ext. 477 or 474

To Marta
for joy

CONTENTS

INTRODUCTION by Charlotte Gray

"MEMORY IS, finally, all we own." When I reached that sentence on the last page of Ernest Hillen's first book, I felt both the joy of coming to the end of a wonderful tale and a profound sadness. Yes, memory might be all we own, but I wanted *more*. More of Ernest's childhood. More of that extraordinarily engaging voice that the adult Ernest had discovered within himself: the voice of a young boy who is both innocent and knowing, truthful and canny. More of the intimate glimpses of a world long gone. In other words, more of Ernest's memories.

The Way of a Boy chronicled a childhood spent in Japanese internment camps in Indonesia—or the Dutch East Indies, as it was then known. From the age of eight, for three and a half years, Ernest was surrounded by Dutch women and children all engaged in the same struggle: to survive, with dignity, even laughter, despite hunger, disease, deprivation, and sadistic guards. Many of the friends young Ernest made in the camps during the years 1942 to 1945 did not survive. Fortunately, the Hillen family did.

As a writer frequently edited by Ernest himself, I knew how good *The Way of a Boy* was. I recalled Ernest's agonizing struggle to recapture those memories by delving deep into his forgotten past. After long days of mining his own psyche, he had then begun the equally demanding process of writing. "I just plowed

ll the speed of a turtle," he says. "The com-
port just 72 or 95 or 163 usable words per ten-
y. And even those few words would often prove not
er all." The quiet, apparently effortless grace of that
r was the culmination of many months of work.

Readers recognized that his "little book," as he called it
with typical self-deprecation, was much bigger than a collec-
tion of random recollections. Every chapter held some jewel of
insight into the bravery and even joy of which ordinary people
are capable—despite being under extreme stress. Every character was explored with sympathy and understanding. *The Way
of a Boy* was not a documentary, but it resonated with the ring
of truth. Ernest himself likes to quote some much-treasured
advice on how to write well from the English author Arnold
Bennett: "You must feel more deeply and think more clearly."

The Way of a Boy was rapturously received by critics when it
appeared in 1993 and quickly became a bestseller. Some
reviewers focused on the extraordinary narrative: "A meticulous
and astonishingly vivid recreation of one child's journey from a
kind of paradise—life among the white-skinned 'plantocracy'
of Dutch-ruled Java—into a kind of hell," wrote a *Globe and Mail*
critic. "At times sad, yet never the least bit sentimental." Other
reviewers focused on Ernest's lyrical and evocative prose.
"Moving and horrifying as they are," suggested London's *Sunday
Telegraph*, "the gentleness and innocent freshness of these recollections are what stay in the mind … entrancing."

Readers like me, however, had a much simpler reaction. We
were hungry for the next installment. *Small Mercies* takes up the
story in 1945, when eleven-year-old Ernest, alongside his
mother and brother, Jerry, sail away from Indonesia at the end
of the war. By the time *Small Mercies* draws to a close with

another sea voyage, in 1947, Ernest has drifted towards the adult world of jobs, drink, and girls—and yet has retained both his mischievous humour and his innocent sweetness.

The end of the Second World War did not bring an end to the challenges facing the Hillen family. Ernest's Dutch father, John, was eager to stay in his beloved Indonesia, but the Indonesian independence movement made Java a dangerous place for colonial expatriates. Puzzled, Ernest watched his mother, Anna, who had demonstrated such grit in the internment camp, mutely concede to John's authority and agree that he should stay on Java while she took responsibility for their two sons. Because Anna was Canadian, John decided that his family should join her relatives there. Canada, he told his sons, was *"een land van melk en honing"* (a land of milk and honey).

In March 1946, the Hillen threesome, full of excitement and anticipation, stepped off a train in Toronto's brightly lit, high-ceilinged Union Station.

Today, it is difficult for us to envisage Canada's largest city without the glittering developments and surge of immigrants of the past half-century. But when Ernest arrived in 1946, there was no curved City Hall, no Toronto Zoo, no CN Tower, no glass bank buildings, no opera house, and certainly no exploding crystal enveloping the dignified Royal Ontario Museum. The city's population was 680,000, only one-fifth of what it is today, and Chinatown was tiny: you rarely heard any language other than English on the badly lit streets. Everything shut down on Sundays because attendance at church (usually Protestant) was virtually compulsory. The English writer Wyndham Lewis, who visited Toronto during the war, called the city "a sanctimonious ice-box." As its longtime citizen Northrop Frye, the literary

.ked to say, Toronto was a good place to mind your own
.ess.

In other words, postwar Toronto might have seemed dull
and its tight-fisted probity confusing for an eleven-year-old
expecting milk and honey. But not for Ernest: after the dark
years of deprivation and ignorance, he embraced the promise
of this frosty land. The Ernest Hillen of *Small Mercies* is older
and more watchful than the child we met in the earlier volume,
and in other circumstances, that child might never have grown
beyond the brutalities he witnessed during the war. In Canada,
however, the boy left the camp far behind, thanks to the opti-
mism and good sense his mother radiated. He was able to play
out the existence of a normal adolescent in an ordinary place.
In *Small Mercies*, there is none of the high drama of wartime in
an occupied country. But there are small mercies—individual
acts of kindness, quiet miracles of sensation, above all, a sense
of sanctuary.

By the time John Hillen summoned his little family back to
Indonesia, Ernest was reluctant to leave his new home in North
America. Too soon, he found himself bouncing around in the
back of a Jeep in Java, as his father drove them alongside a
corpse-strewn canal towards the city that Dutch merchants had
named Batavia in 1619, and was now known as Jakarta.

Small Mercies, published in 1997, was as well received as *The Way
of a Boy*. In the *Toronto Star*, John Fraser described it as "a beau-
tifully crafted little masterpiece." It won The Viacom Canada
Writers' Trust Non-Fiction Award. "One of the most difficult
things a writer can do," read the jury citation, "is return to the
language, the emotions, the inchoate sexuality, and the sometimes lucid, sometimes murky perceptions of a child. Hillen

does so masterfully ... This memoir does more than recall a past. It reclaims it, and with no device other than unerringly beautiful writing."

There was talk of a film of Ernest's memoirs and perhaps a third volume. After all, the story wasn't finished. In 1952, at age seventeen, Ernest had returned to Canada. In subsequent years, he held about thirty different jobs (including an early stint as pastry chef at the Banff Springs Hotel) as he zigzagged his way into this country's literary life. In his late teens he had begun to read voraciously. Books fired his ambition to write, despite his limited education and the fact that he hadn't learned English until he was eleven. Most of all, Ernest wanted to write fiction. Between 1955 and 1958, he was already writing plays that were performed on CBC Radio. "It was all seat-of-the-pants stuff," he recalls. "I killed myself putting sentences together because I had so little control over English in those early years." He gradually developed that control.

By the time I met Ernest in the late 1980s, when we both worked for *Saturday Night* magazine, he was well known in journalism circles for his impressive writing and editing skills. But there was more to his story than professional accomplishments. There were important friendships. (Most women, I have discovered, adore Ernest's company: he *listens* to us. Maybe that is due to those formative years in the exclusively female world of the internment camp.) As he and I became closer friends, he would relate to me some of his past adventures—adventures that, in Ernest's telling, were brought to life by carefully observed detail and a fine understanding of the human heart.

Ernest remained close to his parents, although they were often living far apart. With advancing age, Anna and John Hillen moved into the ground floor of the Toronto house where

Ernest lived with his wife, Marta Tomins. John had reinvented himself as a museum designer and worked on large installations at the Royal Ontario Museum. He died in 1994. Anna spent many years in charge of the children's book section in the Albert Britnell Book Shop, the independent bookstore that once held sway in downtown Toronto at Bloor and Yonge. She finally retired when she was seventy-nine, to help Ernest and Marta raise their daughter, Maia. A book lover throughout her life, Anna, in her final years, read and reread with undiminished pleasure her son's two books. When Ernest walked past her door, she would often look up and say with a smile, "Yes … I'd forgotten … That did happen."

From time to time, I would prod Ernest about a projected third volume of memoirs. Our conversations always took place over the telephone: "How is it going?" I would ask. At first, he would reluctantly mutter, "Slowly …" Then my nagging was met with longer and longer silences. He had health problems, but there was something else, too. "I think I had drained myself," he now suggests. "Maybe I was tired of being so absorbed in myself. Perhaps I had said it all in those two books."

He had, indeed, said so much in his two books. In the camps and in Toronto, his younger self had absorbed lessons that are implicit in the way he tells his story. He had learned never to take anything for granted—relationships, jobs, possessions—and to dismiss pettiness, self-pity, and bullying. He learned that being judgmental of others is usually pointless: you should just get on with living. And he has given us two perfectly rendered memoirs that show how, in the midst of hunger, fear, monotony, and meanness, a child can discover love, courage, humour, and grace.

The main character in both *The Way of a Boy* and *Small Mercies* is, of course, Ernest himself—aren't we all central to our own stories? But it is impossible to read these books without realizing Ernest's debt to his mother. I met Anna only once, at a launch party for *The Way of a Boy*. I recall a small, dignified woman whose proud gaze never left her son. A few years later, Ernest wrote a piece about her in *The Globe and Mail*. Anna's ninety-fourth birthday was on September 12, 2001, the day after the al-Qaeda attacks on New York's twin towers. She had recently been hospitalized after a stroke; Ernest, along with his wife and daughter, had gone to visit her. They didn't mention the previous day's murderous events to her because, Ernest wrote, "She doesn't like big stories anymore. The alert brown eyes wander off, or they close. She likes hearing small things she can nod at and smile about serenely. My wife, Marta, and daughter, Maia, fifteen, are superb at coming up with those; I don't know how to talk to my mother that way."

"But let's say she'd known about the eleventh—it happened here! it could have been us!—[but she would also have felt] a kind of pensive wistfulness … I think she might have felt that our collective 'experience' was, possibly, one small mercy hidden inside all the horror—the forging of a sad link with the rest of the world."

Anna died a few months later. Years earlier, on another continent in another era, she had passed on to her son her belief in the essence of a common humanity. This belief, captured in limpid prose, is what characterizes Ernest Hillen's remarkable memoirs.

SMALL
MERCIES

ONE / Small Mercies

IT WAS TOO DARK TO SEE, but over the steady hum in that small space I heard her slow breathing. I was restless. It was late, probably past ten. Though she was fairly easy about night hours, I let myself drop out of bed silent as a snake anyway. She made a little moan and I froze in a crouch on the trembling floor—she couldn't have heard me. Soundlessly I dressed by touch. When I eased the door open, only one light was still on in the passageway. I ran down its lightly swaying length, up carpeted stairs, and through a door the wind slammed shut behind me. I undid my sandals and under the stars trotted off to my steel cave.

The "cave" was a shallow covered niche at the tip of the MS *Devonshire's* bow where the grey ship's sides joined and curved up into a beak that arched over where far below she sliced the water. From here, during the day, I could keep an eye on things—derricks, cables, lifeboats, decks, the towering bridge with its many framed eyes, and the two massive funnels; at night, lights dimly outlined the ship's form or, in fog, floated bobbing and swinging on their own. The nook held only a coil of frayed rope so, knees-up, head-down, I just fitted. The throbbing from the engines didn't reach there, nor the moaning from the air ducts, nor the push of the wind. One of the remotest spots on board, though liable to every shudder and pitch—crazily in a storm, it was a good place to think.

I jogged forward from shadow to shadow. The decks were deserted except for the odd soldier leaning against a railing, smoking, gazing out to sea. Going home, he was, alive. I stayed clear of them and of open portholes, slid down steel bannisters, and sprinted the upsloping last stretch of deck to get to my hole unseen by those standing watch inside the strange blue light of the bridge.

Squatting in the stillness, I let my mind wander. I didn't want to think. I put off most real thinking. I used to think a lot just a few months ago—well, what I did was sit in shadowy places, staring, dopily turning over and over fancies about food; I was, I suppose, a bit dead. But those days were fading and I let them. Real thinking would come when my mind stopped boiling. Instead, impatiently, I "floated" from my crunched position in the bow to just above the bridge, hovered there, then soared straight up until the ship below was just a few lights pulling a white belt through the dark. I'd moved like a spirit but didn't think of myself as one; I stayed me. When I was very young, Manang, our gardener, had told me about spirits—spirits inside people and animals, in the air, on mountains, and in trees where during storms the souls of children cried; it only made sense that there would be spirits at sea as well.

The "floating" was a wonderful trick I had invented that first hectic day on board—so I could dash over, in my mind, to a spot from which I had a completely different view. It could be anywhere, up in the air, on any deck, on the bridge if I liked. It let me survey the ship from every angle, on it and off it. Several times, for example, I'd even "visited" the Captain's cabin. I would never actually set foot there, but was pretty sure what it looked like inside. A friend of mine who was alive, Zuseke Crone, had a husband who was a ship's captain; she'd shown me his picture. The small room in the crowded house she and her three children lived in had been very neat but not *gezellig* (an important word in Dutch, meaning cozy, comfortable, homey, friendly, cheerful). I imagined at the time that's also what Mr. Crone's cabin looked like, and so, too, the *Devonshire* Captain's cabin—neat but not *gezellig*. It was in the dining room, where you could eat as much as you wanted, that I discovered that not only could I "float," but then I could look back at *myself* as well. An invisible me watching the real me from another table, from the ceiling, through a porthole—marvellous. "Floating" gave me a spirit's freedom all right, yet I didn't do it much: it felt a little scary. Besides, I was on a mighty voyage to a distant land with a sweet brown name that sounded like chocolate. The real me had enough to do on the ship. On the go. On the run.

Today was December 13, 1945; on December 10 we'd boarded the *Devonshire* in Singapore; the chart under glass in the cocktail lounge showed three sailing days plotted. Only four months ago—sometimes it seemed like four years, sometimes four days—I'd been "a bit dead" one day, and then the next day "shocks" had started coming, a few big ones, then little ones, dozens and dozens of shocks, coming faster and faster, blurring into one another. They came, I guess, just in time. I stuck my head out of the cave and tasted the salty air. Foam glinting at their crests, fat black waves rolled into darkness.

It was evening. Some three thousand of us, bony women and children pocked with sores, in rags, stood assembled on a field of red mud fenced in by barbed wire while above us like a cloud hung the stink of our shit—and right then a trumpet should have blared, lightning should have cracked! After three and a half years of imprisonment we needn't bow to the enemy any more. The enemy, we were told, had surrendered! But, instead of joy, there was an instant shushing and the head of Camp Makasar, another prisoner, warned us not to yell, not to raise the flag, not to sing the national anthem. She said that, because our camp was so near Batavia (Jakarta, on Java), Indonesians living there might hear us. Indonesia may have been the Dutch East Indies when the Japanese invaded in 1942, but it was known that the moment the Japanese capitulated Indonesians meant to fight us, the Dutch, to get their country back. If we were attacked, our guards sure weren't going to do any protecting and Allied troops hadn't landed yet. So, to mark the war's end, we were permitted two minutes of silence.

A few people cried, but most, like my mother, just stood there, like stones. My best friend, Hubie van Boxel, who had golden hair (that's the word people used, golden) had died two weeks earlier absolutely certain—as I was—that the war would never end. It made sense. We'd simply been forgotten and those of us still living would stay in camp and die there, one a little faster than another, but everybody would get their turn, children, too, curled up in small bamboo coffins. Trudging back to our barrack with my mother in the dark I knew what she'd say next; they were about the only English words I understood then. And sure enough, inside barrack 4A, after she'd loosened her long red hair and we lay side by side on our narrow lousy mattresses scratching, she whispered, "Well, dammit—thank God for small mercies!" It's what she always said after a "fluke," a piece of luck, big or small, it didn't matter, and often included an English curse. She swore a little; I did, too.

4

Food rations had grown so small over the years, adults said, that the mid-August liberation had come none too soon; six months later we'd all have been dead. But, the very next morning extra rice was suddenly distributed, and then we raced back laughing into other line-ups for—unbelievably!—oil, fruit, sugar, soap, and *toothpaste*. And two days later a British plane thundered in low over Makasar dropping boxes swinging from parachutes—canned food, milk powder, medicine, cigarettes, *chocolate*. And the day after that, British officers, *looking* shocked, wandered around inspecting Makasar. And then, one afternoon ten days later, my father walked into camp.

Was it my father? I hadn't seen him since he and the other white men from our tea plantation had been trucked away to men's camps three and a half years earlier; women and children had followed a few weeks later, to other camps. A smaller man, round-shouldered, he hugged me and said, "I'm your father." "Yes, sir," I answered. His eyes tried to look inside my head like they used to, but it didn't work any more. He called me *jongetje*, "little boy" in Dutch, but I didn't feel like a *jongetje* any more. His last words to my brother, Jerry, and me had been, "Look after your mother." His blue-grey eyes had burned into our brown ones. Well, maybe Jerry, who was eleven then, knew what he meant, but I was seven, and had no idea. It was a strange thing to say. How could a little kid take care of his mom? Make her laugh? Bring her tea? It didn't make sense. She was there to take care of me.

"Jerry?" she and I wanted to know right away. My father said he was just fine. Jerry had been with us in women's camps in the city of Bandung (where she and I were interned longest) until, at thirteen, he and boys his age were taken away, we didn't know

where, because the Japanese thought they'd become a "danger to the state." It had puzzled me that when the truck drove off Jerry was grinning: he would be "his own boss," my mother had explained. But by chance he landed in the same camp as our father. When we found out, my mother said lucky us: father and son, mother and son. Well, maybe. Our father liked "discipline," which, it seemed, just meant promptly obeying and not crossing him. Before the war he had taught discipline in many ways, mostly to Jerry as the oldest. So for about a year and a half Jerry had been alone with our father and I thought he might have taken in a lot of discipline.

By the time my father discovered my mother and I were in Makasar, British soldiers had landed on Java and begun policing cities and highways; Dutch troops soon followed. From his and Jerry's camp in Tjimahi, a small town near Bandung, my father had hitchhiked on military vehicles to Batavia. "I would have walked," he told my mother, and that was probably true.

We sat on our mattresses in 4A, my parents holding hands. With his free hand my father took something from an old children's schoolbag he carried, and handed it to her. It was a polished wooden box with lumpy roundings like women's thighs, and fitting inside it, exactly, a carved necklace of dozens of finely smoothed balls the size of peanuts; set apart by even smaller balls was a pendant of two maple leaves and an open acorn with, inside it, a third maple leaf. What my father had worked with, I'm sorry to say, I didn't ask—a razor-blade, glass-slivers, sand, who knows: he had no tools. He'd made these beautiful things from the roots of some hardwood bush, in secret, to give to my mother, "If, Anna," he said to her then, eyes blinking, "we lived." The maple leaves were because she was from Canada. My mother whispered, "Oh, John." I looked at her looking at him.

I wouldn't be missed, so I wandered outside. All through the camps she'd talked about him, stories, little details, also about Jerry after he was taken away, and about relatives in Canada and Holland; she marked their birthdays: "It's fun," she'd say. "This is how we'll survive." She'd told me how once upon a time the two of them had met. In the summer of 1929, two young Dutchmen, Jan Hillen and Gerard Röling, an artist, had crossed the Atlantic to make a long-planned Canadian canoe trip from someplace in southern Ontario all the way up to James Bay. They had been paddling for a month through endless hot mosquito-infested bush when the banks of the small river they were on suddenly changed to lawn. Then, high up one side, they spied two red-haired young women carrying a basket of oranges. The grubby, unshaven Dutchmen waved and shouted. The women looked over, one stumbled, the basket tipped, and oranges bounded down to the water. The Dutchmen raced yipping for shore. Sloshing after oranges, they learned they were in vacation country, in Muskoka, on a cottager's private grounds; the redheads were public-school teachers just starting a week's holiday. The men promptly hauled in the canoe and asked permission to pitch camp, their journey, it seems, done and over. The four had age in common, twenty-two, and by the end of the week Gerard Röling had become good friends with one redhead—and Jan Hillen had asked the other, Anna Watson, to marry him.

Perhaps it was the smell of Camp Makasar's open latrines— she and I were used to it—but my father told us we were going to take the first train back to Bandung next day, a three-hour run from Batavia: trains were probably safe. There was no discussion. Even though she was an adult and proud of her "common sense," my mother had always discussed decisions with us in camp. Now her serious brown eyes watched this restless man, blond hair combed back flat, often sighing—who knew why—and wordlessly she agreed. I had no say at all. Bring the minimum, my father instructed, all would be provided in Tjimahi. There wasn't much to leave behind: our mattresses, some grey worn-out sheets, a mosquito net covered in bug blood, two spoons, a fork, two mugs, and a lidded can for sugar. I owned a pair of shorts, a short-sleeved shirt, a harmonica, a khaki-cloth rucksack, and, especially given to me by his mother, Hubie's riding boots, a beret, and a toy soldier on a horse. My mother had a skirt and a shirt for working in, some underwear including a tea-towel-brassiere, one dress, and sandals.

Next morning, barefoot between my parents, I walked out of Makasar's barbed-wire gate. A whistling English soldier standing guard gave us a little salute. I was barefoot because I wouldn't wear Hubie's boots: his mother had hoarded them for *him* to walk out in. My mother wore the green dress and sandals she'd saved for this day—this day we'd pictured a thousand times. Just a short way beyond the gate, under a suddenly soaring sky, in air suddenly fresh and wind suddenly touching, there ran a wide pitted dusty road—bell-ringing carrier tricyles and bicycles, screaking horse-drawn carriages, honking trucks and, on the sidewalks, fluttery women in tight sarongs, children holding hands, yelling vendors, all moving unhurriedly, a few Chinese, mostly Indonesians. Lots of them thin, poorly dressed, even in rags, but all with purposes—and free. Unseen and unheard, that traffic had rambled to and fro all our dead days.

But this was just another day for the road—and we were the only whites on it. In camp, rumours had flared of armed Indonesians forcing *orang Blanda*, us Dutch, to stay in camps, of torture and killings. But no one on the road paid us any attention. My father waved down a Jeep driven by a soldier, a turbaned one called a Sikh, and asked in English for a ride to Batavia's railway station. The Sikh nodded without turning. We climbed in, my father up front, my mother and I in back, me behind my father—and I locked my eyes for dear life on the Sikh. A single look down that go-as-you-please road had been enough. For three and a half years, eight-foot plaited-bamboo walls had blocked my eyes, but in the Jeep I couldn't look. The road and then the city's hot streets sped by in a whir of colours and shapes—and smells: fried banana, roasted meat—but I fixed on the Sikh. The sun was nearly white, yet his uniform shirt was done up to the throat, sleeves buttoned down, beard pressed to his chin in a hairnet. On his left wrist he wore a copper bracelet; a walkie-talkie hung from an epaulet, a holstered revolver from his belt. Tall and lean with a thin, curved nose, he sat rigidly behind the wheel, black eyes ahead, never speaking. I didn't want to look at him any more, but didn't dare watch the world: it was too open. Outside the station my father thanked the Sikh, who nodded once and drove off.

Inside, Indonesians carting baskets, chickens, and babies scurried amidst whistles, shouts, and shrieking steel—and I homed in on the rear ends of my hand-holding parents. My father pushed into a line-up for tickets, then ran us to a far platform where we hoisted ourselves into a second-class coach, just in time; on two facing benches in the fourth compartment three seats were free. Five more people jammed in behind us,

Indonesian women and a high-voiced man, the only other white I saw; they'd have to stand. During the trip, though, my father, or I at his look, would offer to let a woman or Mr. Bilt sit for a while. Doing strangers favours for free, I thought, was just dumb. The women, small and cool and neat, smiled but said thank you, no, *tuan,* "sir." Mr. Bilt always piped yes. In my mind I took the "t" off Bilt so he became *Meneer Bil,* "Mr. Ass" in Dutch.

My first train trip had occurred before the war, grandly alone at night in the locomotive all the way from Bandung to a depot near the plantation; the engineer had let me yank away at the whistle cord. During the war, my mother and I had travelled from Bandung to Batavia locked in a pitch-dark, fourth-class coach packed with other prisoners; the three-hour run became twenty, and we all did it in our pants. On *this* ride, we passed through tender-green rice fields dotted with farmers in conical hats driving water buffalo and, on higher ground, small bamboo houses, coconut trees, clumps of jungle growth. Glittering in the sun, the watery fields climbed terrace by terrace into hazy purple hills which, as we chugged further inland, swelled into hazy purple mountains. Our open window let in a little breeze, and soot and live embers. At the many small-station stops, my father leaned out and bargained with pedlars for water, bananas, papaya slices, rambutans; no cookies, cookies were expensive. A man with a big silvery tin hanging from his neck sold ice lollies, red, green, blue, white. Even after so long, I could *taste* them, but no, fruit was better for you. We passengers sat or stood rocking and bumping against one another, skin wetly touching skin, trying to doze.

Then, in the middle of nowhere, the train screeched to a stop. Eyes flew open and we lunged for the window. Up and down the train other heads poked out and in the sudden stillness we heard bird cries and the locomotive puffing. We sat or stood very straight, watched each other, listened. A door slammed at the end of the corridor, angry voices, yelling, a scream, scuffling, then slaps: familiar sounds—*stay calm; yield.* The commotion drew closer. Our compartment door slammed open and hard-breathing young Indonesians crowded in, *"Identifikasi! Identifikasi!"* Long-haired as women, they smelled wild and their skin shivered. Rifles hung from small shoulders, machetes from belts. Barefoot, they wore ripped, dirt-caked clothes but fresh white red-lettered headbands. The letters probably spelled MERDEKA! "Freedom!" the favourite slogan of what we called the Extremists. They at once picked out us whites.

"Identifikasi!"

My father stood up, bowed slightly, offered a pink card politely with both hands, and nodded towards my mother and me to show we were with him. Mr. Bilt, the idiot, had his card out but wouldn't pass it over—*their* identification first, he shrilled, a Dutchman not taking guff. For a moment it was very quiet—until my father jerked around, snatched Mr. Bilt's card away, and handed it over. *"Ezel!"* he said quietly to Mr. Bilt in Dutch. "Donkey!" The armed men studied the cards, tossed them back, and swaggered out to the next compartment. After a little while, the locomotive whistled and the train lurched forward. On a narrow dyke between rice fields the slender men trotted away single file towards the hills. Staring after them, my father, frowning, muttered something to himself. In the next few weeks I'd overhear him and other white men discuss the Extremists, in a soothing adult way, as rascals who simply needed discipline. They, the Dutch, were as keen as always, they said, to help Indonesians "mature" and, of course, as soon as

Indonesians had done so, would be glad to hand them back their country. But first things first. Indonesia badly needed fixing and they, the Dutch, had spent 350 years doing just that. The fighting spread, though, and white patience ran out—the rebels simply needed squashing. There would be other adventures with Freedom Fighters, as *they* called themselves, but what stayed with me from what happened on the train was my father's fine quick action.

At one point, sitting swaying across from me, he leaned over and placed his hands on my knees, eyes glowing like a child's. From the time he'd walked into camp the day before, my mother had mostly absorbed him, but now, it seemed, it was my turn; my mother sitting back had her eyes closed. He was really a stranger to me though. Just as almost overnight the prison camp's crowded life had smothered the memory of our quiet plantation, so, too, had it pressed out the memory of him. My mother tried to keep it alive, sure, but soon I couldn't *see* him. I'd remembered his able hands—drawing or repairing things, spanking Jerry with a thin leather slipper, or oh so gently letting down the gramophone's needle on a record. He read a lot, like my mother and Jerry; and he had been keen on discipline. The rest was really information from my mother. He liked English (that's how Jerry and I got our names and why we called him "Daddy"); he loved his sons, music, painting, sailing, and motorcycling; he worked hard, was strict but fair, had travelled a lot, spoke fluent Dutch, English, German, and Indonesian, couldn't dance, and was sometimes funny—remember how on the plantation he and Uncle Fred at either end of the dining-room table had flipped fried eggs back and forth? I looked down at the short, strong hands on my knees; the right index finger was stained yellow. Boxes on parachutes had probably also dropped into Camp Tjimahi; he must have smoked a lot since.

Softly, warmly, my father said to me that he knew that I had had it tough, yes?

Wrapped inside his attention, I felt my face grow hot: it was the first time in years that a man was speaking to me, deep rumbling for just my ears. Aside from barking guards, the last man to talk to me had been Mr. Otten with the little moustache. Mr. Otten had shot a wild boar on the plantation and given me its head to bury and later, cleaned by worms, to dig up as a beautiful white skull to put in my room. That was just before we were interned; deep down in the red earth, teeth grinning, the skull had to be there still. My eyes stayed on my father's hands. *What* had been tough?

Oh yes, my father said, *tough,* and he sighed.

For his finger to get that yellow, he must've smoked a tin a day.

My mother, my father said, had told him that I'd grown up a lot as a person. A lot, he said again. He had been pleased— yes, even proud—to hear that. Of course, he had observed that himself the moment he laid eyes on me.

Meaning? A week ago she'd slapped my face; only the second slap in all those years, but still. "Don't you dare look at girls or women like that," she'd snapped. I'd been staring at bare legs and at breasts. She didn't blab though. So what *had* he noticed? That I could pass by sick and dying people and not *see* them? That I *knew* that pain was just pain and death just death?

Still, my father went on quietly, it was important that I not forget that I *was* a boy—the finger touched my chin—and boys, even boys who'd grown up a lot, Ernest, *listened* to their fathers, looked them in the eye.

The blue-grey eyes were waiting.

Even though I was young, my father said, it was important for me to know that the war had also been tough for *him*, Daddy. *Extremely* tough. As head of the family it had perhaps been *toughest* for him. He'd had Jerry to care for. He'd had my mother and me and the future to worry about. All that had been *his* burden. He sighed. Did I understand what he was saying?

I nodded.

He wanted me to think about that, my father said, his voice a little strained. Yes, I should think about how tough it had been for him. How lonely. I should think about it hard.

My God—*tears!* I nodded and nodded.

His wet eyes shone. Then he swallowed, took a deep breath, and said that the awful suffering was now behind him. And yes, behind *all* of us. We Hillens were going to be a family again. We Hillens were going to live good and normal lives and live them in a safe and quiet place. Now, he said, I should listen closely. What he was going to say was *very serious.* Was I listening?

I nodded, nodded.

He had already spoken of it to Jerry. He and Jerry, he said, had had many fine talks—Jerry listened; he wanted to have fine talks with me, too, of course. Did I realize that I was going to go to school one day soon? Well, I was. And when I was in school he expected me to work hard, very hard, no excuses, so that I would catch up fast after the years in camp with no school. And this— a light press on my knees—was the reason why: he wanted *me*, Ernest, to make *him*, Daddy, *proud* of me. But, he warned, it would take a lot—*a great deal*—to make him proud.

That was it. He'd had something to say in the shaking railway car that he'd wanted me to hear and then his attention shut off like a lamp. I didn't mind; hadn't minded when it was on either. I hadn't understood much, but that was all right: he might say it again. Smiling a bit sadly, my father slumped back on his bench and shut his eyes.

As we clattered through high country towards Bandung it grew less humid and less hot. The city lay in a valley but I remembered that you could shiver in the rain there, that at night in mountain homes people lit hearth fires. We'd lived in Bandung for short spells before the war and then in three camps—residential sections walled off by bamboo and barbed wire. Few city sounds had reached inside the camps and contact with the outside (mostly to smuggle food) was forbidden— the Japanese beat up, shaved the heads of, and killed internees for breaking rules. So, after a while, Bandung had stopped being real and we forgot we lived inside it.

We steamed into the city as an orange sun sank away and it promptly turned dark. Ours must have been the day's last train because, once the other passengers had scuttled off, the dimly lit station grew still; even small sounds rebounded from the high ceiling. Long neglect showed in cracked walls, broken windows, thickets of spider webs; a few human forms in rags sprawled in corners. My father at once hurried off to find transportation to Tjimahi and for the first time since he'd come to fetch us my mother and I were alone.

We'd been on our own a long time. She'd always had to work during the day—all adults and teenagers did—but evenings we talked or were quiet together until lights-out. I thought I knew her well. But, maybe not. She'd changed since my father's arrival. I was used to her eyes often looking, even in conversation, as if she were far away—thinking, dreaming. She'd give you lots of her attention, but not all of it. That was fine: the "look" was one of her ways "of taking care of myself." So, too, was reading into the night, when books were still permitted, and to hell with lights-out. Or insisting, when she came home from work, on being alone for a while—"That's how I restore myself." Or never sharing, as some mothers did, her food rations with me because, she said, those women risked illness, then death, and leaving their kids orphans. All through the camps she'd taken care by being cautious, accepting people and situations as they were, and using her "common sense" which was linked to her be-true-to-yourself rule (endlessly urged on me) which, really, meant being your *best* self. But when she saw my father the "look" went away. And, as the hours passed and the two of them laughed and talked, often in English to be private, and the three of us travelled, it didn't return, and it wouldn't in the days and weeks ahead. Her eyes were very alert. My father needed all her attention.

In the quiet station I felt his absence, how *there* he was when he was. I pulled on Hubie's boots, finally feeling it was okay now; stomped them down making an echo: a perfect fit. From the station's tracks rose the same smell as in Makasar; insects whirred and thrummed. The green dress hung on her; she'd worn it last on the first Christmas Day in camp when, the only non-Dutch person there, she'd ended up singing, alone and off-key, "Hark the Herald Angels Sing," and had run away crying. I hadn't seen her cry again. I clumped around dragging my feet, "sloff-sloffing" like Japanese officers did in their boots. She watched: yes, that's how they'd moved all right.

I asked her if Jerry would still be the same old Jerry.

She wasn't a mother who touched a lot, but then she took my cheeks between her hands and softly squeezed a fishmouth. Yes, she said smiling, Jerry would be same old Jerry when we saw him tonight. But he would be *more*.

How?

He would be wiser.

Why?

Because, she said, letting my face go, Jerry had been "his own boss" for a long time.

What about Daddy?

Daddy had been there, yes. And Daddy would certainly have kept an eye on Jerry. All the same, Jerry had been on his own a lot, too. He hadn't had me, or her, after all. Also, knowing Jerry, he would have kept an eye on Daddy, right?

True. Jerry had always watched out for me, even her.

Would he be awake when we got to Tjimahi?

Oh yes.

I had another question, not asked sooner because we hadn't been alone. Were we, I wanted to know, really free now?

She looked around the quiet building. The shapes in the shadows didn't stir. She swung her arms sideways, fluttered her hands, and like an airplane, but standing still, looped this way and that, as Jerry and I used to do playing pilots. Yes, she laughed, oh yes, oh hell yes, you bet, we really were damn well free!

I had to ask though: Weren't we going to just another camp in Tjimahi? With a fence? With rules?

Sure, but it would be temporary.

Were the English going to shoot the Japs? *All* the Japs?

No, she didn't think so.

Why *not*? They'd beaten us. Starved us. Killed us. Hubie was dead. We could've all . . .

She held up her hand, frowning—until the words were ready. That's just how she'd looked once very early on in camp. She'd had an important message then, and repeated it so Jerry and I would remember. "The Japanese soldiers," she'd told us, "have guns and they are dangerous. They don't like you, even if they smile at you. We are their enemy and if we disobey them or get in their way they will kill us. Always be polite, always be serious, always stay calm. Don't laugh, don't smile, don't joke. Don't look them in the eye. I am afraid and I know that you are afraid. But you'll be less afraid if you remember what I'm telling you." Now in Bandung station she said slowly, "We were at war, but it's over. Get it through your head—the war is over. Put it behind you. Get on with life. Get on to the next damn adventure! And understand: it was Japanese military men who made us suffer—not a whole nation." And in the days to come, in different words and every chance she got, she'd hammer this new message home—to me, to Jerry, to herself, and perhaps also to my father.

I turned sharply away and in my new boots marched eyes ahead, chest out—as Jerry had done in soft rain the last time I saw him. At the far end of the platform, where rusted tracks below cut through high weeds and ran off into the dark, I jumped around and standing very straight screamed *"Keirei!"*— the command "Bow!" in Japanese. The building boomed *"Keirei!"* back, but I didn't move a muscle.

The *Devonshire* had begun to pitch and for me, curled up inside the bow's steel cave, there came with each leap a moment of weightlessness. I rose, floated, fell. I stuck out a leg and the wind tugged at it. Spatterings hit the deck. The stars still stood clear but, whipped on by cords of foam, the earlier fat slow waves had turned lean and fast. With the sea's mood switch there came my usual little urge—to jump overboard and swim away. Night and day, calm or rough, the water invited. If land was in sight, even a speck, I was sure I could reach it swimming, and if no land, well, another ship would show up, or something. Anyhow, I'd been told that because of the salt the sea was much lighter to swim in than fresh water—so I could always drift. I hadn't actually swum since I was seven. On the plantation we swam every day; it was never denied. Every morning, before lunch, all the white families strolled up to the swimming pool. It was the choice spot on the estate: from it you could see all our houses, the soccer field, the factory, the main road. On weekends we took picnic baskets and spent almost entire days there. Jerry and I had few toys, but every day held the certainty of play in the pool. On birthdays we jumped in with our clothes on. If it rained, our mother said that was all the more reason to go. In bed I planned amazing jumps and tricks for the next day. Eyes wide open beneath the surface lit by the sun I could make the pool's length under water back and forth. I could *see* now my excellent dive from the ship: on tiptoe from the bow, the stern, wherever, a long swooping one that knifed the warm water and let me glide deep, eyes open, safe, free.

On the wet heaving decks the return to midships took longer. I seemed to be all alone except for shapes moving in the bridge's eerie light; there they never slept. The wind fought opening B-Deck's steel outside door. Inside, at the foot of the stairs, I looked down our corridor. The doors were identical, but numbered—15B was ours, and never locked. I opened it, stepped in, shut it soundlessly. The reading light in the lower bunk was now on. My mother had wakened but wouldn't have worried about me. Covered by a sheet to her chin she lay with eyes closed, hair loose, a book open on her chest. I lifted the book, laid it on the floor, and shut off the light. I undressed and climbed into the top bunk, straightening slowly so the springs stayed quiet. From below she mumbled, Ridiculous hours. . . .

The cabin hummed and, with the ship's moves, softly creaked. She always left the porthole ajar and when that side of the *Devonshire* rolled close to the sea's surface I could hear foam hissing.

TWO / Bright Passages

IT SEEMED THAT EVERY DAY the *Devonshire* steamed along afloat in light. The sun was one source, flooding down and flashing back off the water and, in the sea wind, never mean. For years, it had been a friend only of the Japanese. Even their flag was white with a red sun in the middle; Jerry had hated it, didn't want to see it. The Japanese used the sun to hurt us. Day in day out they let it burn down on workers, weakening and dulling them. A prisoner who broke a rule might be dragged to a shadeless spot to stand at attention, or sit there hunched up in a little bamboo cage, for a day, or two days, eyes burning, lips cracking, with no food or water and kicks and slaps if she blacked out. The other source of light on the ship, though, was the passengers. They glowed—that is the word for it—so brightly sometimes that it seemed that all of them, not just the ship's officers, were dressed in white. They glowed as they ate, drank, read, talked, laughed, strolled, wrestled, danced, wrote letters, dozed in deck chairs, played cards, did anything really. They lit up the ship. And they could all have been dead.

Lying in my bunk fully dressed, I watched through the porthole as early morning turned a calm-again sea pure silver. I felt a bit jumpy, as I did every morning, because every new day promised so *much*—and the whole damn ship was waiting upstairs! I couldn't leave yet though. Any moment a steward would come by in the corridor tapping his little copper gong with a velvet drumstick: first-sitting breakfast. That soft dinging ruled the ship's slow hours absolutely, because breakfast, lunch, and dinner did; the sound also soothed an itch of worry I still had before every meal—would it be there?

On day one, after boarding the *Devonshire* at dawn in Singapore, we'd been served a huge welcome breakfast, the only meal on the ship my mother and Jerry and I would share: stewards in white jackets, tablecloths, plates without cracks, cups with ears—and all you could eat of white and brown bread, buns, butter, porridge, brown and white sugar, marmalade, strawberry jam, raspberry jam, honey, peanut butter, tea, coffee, milk, orange juice, eggs, bacon, ham, sausages, and sliced papaya. A breakfast-as-usual, it turned out, but from then on my mother ate with officers and women in the dining room, Jerry with soldiers in a mess hall, and I with about twenty children in an alcove off the dining room.

Just the three of us boarded; my father had stayed behind in Batavia at his new job. We had only WANTED-ON-VOYAGE baggage and easily lugged it up the gangway ourselves. We owned a lot more, though, than we had in August: several changes of clothes plus *underwear* (something new), sandals, toothbrushes, soap, towels, all from the Red Cross; and our mother had a new watch, Jerry a fountain pen, and I a silver flashlight that could switch from white to red to blue—our first presents, bought, she said, because we "deserved" them. In Singapore that day the *Devonshire* took on another sixty or so civilians, mostly British women and children, and about three thousand British soldiers who'd fought for years in jungles; later, in other ports, we'd pick up a thousand more. And true enough, everybody on board, except maybe the crew, could have been dead. Instead, they were a little tired but alive, lucky souls, and going home.

The gong sounded, and I ran upstairs, in Hubie's riding boots; one of my mother's few rules on the ship—I was never to feel so free again—stipulated, for some reason, footwear at meals and after dark. I peeked in the dining room but, always up earlier, she was still out on one of her fast around-deck walks. Meals were events, and I wished I could eat with the adults: the other children were all small and a bit messy. Still, because they needed care, young nursemaids and mothers sat in with us; their loose-fitting, sleeveless dresses gave nice glimpses of the white sideswells of breasts cupped by brassieres. The women eyed me, too: as the biggest kid, they used me to point up table manners and appetite. So I sat up straight, worked my napkin, never thumbed food or slurped, and regularly overate.

I was as usual first done, but took one more slice of bread, spread on butter, then peanut butter. I should, I felt, show the women something else remarkable about me. On each table sat a silver tray that held pepper, salt, oil, vinegar, and a jar of *sambal oelek*, a fiery red Indonesian condiment prepared from tiny peppers; *sambal* can bring on tears and sweat, but I'd eaten it all my life. I "floated" upward then in my way so I could watch from just above the service door as I reached for the *sambal*, never eaten at breakfast, and lathered it like jam on top of the peanut butter—yes, two of the moms were taking notice. I folded the bread into an oozing sandwich and bit off a mouthful—oh, what a *lusty* appetite! But then the children at my table started whining, and more chimed in around the room, that they now wanted *sambal* on their bread, too. From my perch I could see one mom roll her eyes, the other pull a mouth—damn little *show-off*! Sometimes I got things so wrong.

On the way out, I checked my mother's table again. There she was, eating porridge, chatting with an officer, smiling; she wore a soft green scarf fluffed at her throat. I seldom sought her out and she didn't fuss about me either: I'd been almost on my own, after all, for years. On that ship she behaved as I'd never known her to: all day long, like me, and I thought like Jerry, she simply enjoyed herself. And her eyes had their "look" again. I'd been watching for it and knew exactly when it had come back.

Coming face to face with Jerry again in Camp Tjimahi it was hard not to cry; hard for him, too, I thought, when, wearing his shy crooked grin, he first saw our mother. Jerry wasn't much taller but even more quiet. He had changed and not changed. For about a year and a half he had carried all by himself our father's discipline, but really, the two of them got on fine. I wrestled with thoughts about Jerry. He was as gentle and generous as I remembered, but I noticed he imitated, in gestures, with words, many of our father's ways. Had he been emptied of himself a little? Still, he was my best friend again; the four-year gap between us seemed even to have shrunk and he and I played as I hadn't played since the Japanese had trucked him away.

For about six weeks we lived like "a normal family" in a real house, though shared with others. We got enough to eat, but even so, it was a camp, with rules; outside, angry Extremists roamed. In Tjimahi our parents talked so often in English, arguing as well, it made us a little curious. Then my father flew to Batavia to report for a job with the Dutch government. The three of us followed two weeks later in a Catalina flying boat so noisy inside we couldn't speak. The seatless plane was packed with wounded and sick British soldiers several of whom vomited

(Jerry did too) and a few of whom, even though they were men, even though they covered their eyes, I saw crying . . . *pain.*

Our father had a room waiting for us in the once-famous Hotel der Nederlanden. It had its own shower stall, a broken ceiling fan, and a single bed. Our mother got the bed, Jerry and I mattresses on the floor. Sometimes our father stayed over, and there would be more private talks, but usually he slept in his boarding house. He told us that in the "good old days" when you ordered the hotel's fifty-one-dish *rijsttafel,* a "snake" of fifty-one barefooted waiters in starched white trousers and jackets and golden batik headcloths would come gliding across the dining room, each carrying a single dish on the fingertips of his right hand. But now the hotel's guests, mostly widowers and widows and their children, drooped about in the dusty lobby waiting for passage home to Holland; some had sudden sobbing spells . . . *death.* Here and there, standing still and tall as trees, aloof Sikhs guarded us. I wanted to show Jerry Camp Makasar, just outside Batavia, but no, because of the Extremist "nuisance" we couldn't leave the grounds.

One day after lunch, he and I and two other kids sat watching traffic from the low whitewashed wall that edged the hotel's front lawn. It was the hot still hour when air trembled and cicadas whined loudest. Across the street, half-seen through a hedge of withered banana trees, was a canal stiff with scum. Suddenly we heard a thin whistling—and, as shots cracked, we four had already flung ourselves down behind the wall. How had we *known* to do that? A fast peek over the wall showed banana leaves flapping. They were aiming at us, definitely, from across the canal. More whistling, more shots. Then silence, no cicadas even. Three Sikhs with Sten guns came running up from behind the hotel, bent low, zigzagging, dispersing on the street. Long minutes and no more gunfire. With Jerry leading, the four of us crawled back across the hotel's dry yellow lawn, up cool marble steps, and inside. Somebody had aimed a gun, squeezed a trigger, and tried to kill us. Kill Jerry. Kill *me*!

The next evening in the hotel's buzzing, half-dark dining room our parents told us the big news. That is, he spoke, slowly and low, while she nodded him on and watched us.

What he had to say, our father began, was *very serious*.

He leaned forward—so we had to, also—and lit a Camel. Our round, pink-clothed table became an island. We were a family discussing important matters.

It had been difficult and lonely to make this decision, our father said, and he'd thought about it a long time. But, as a man and as head of the family, well, he'd had no choice.

He said this looking at Jerry, at me, and at our mother, as if she were a third child, as if there had been no secret talks in English, as if the decision, whatever it was, really was his alone. And she just sat there.

Indonesia right now, he said, just wasn't a place for women and children. Too dangerous, too expensive, no proper schools. Many families were returning to Holland for those reasons, but not us. His new job was a good one and he, well, he loved Indonesia, so our future was here. Holland, frankly, was a *kikker-land*, "a land of frogs," too *small*. But he knew that his wife and sons needed to recuperate, needed normal living, needed schooling. That could all be had in Holland, true, but war had devastated Holland, as well. No, until Indonesia settled down, which shouldn't take long—six months, a year—he had made up his mind that he wanted the three of us to live in *een land van melk en honing*.

He looked at our mother, and she gave him a small smile. The cigarette was burning itself out in the ashtray.

He would stay on alone in Batavia, he said. Whatever he'd owned on the plantation—motorcycle, records, books, furniture—was gone, looted. So he'd stay behind, earn money, rent a house, buy beds, cupboards, dishes, and ready a new home for us. He'd have to work *extremely* hard. No recuperation for him.

His strong eyes suddenly bore into mine, then into Jerry's, mine again, back and forth.

Boys, that was called *duty.* A man couldn't shirk it. We should know—and remember this moment—that when we were men we would not shirk duty either.

Jerry was looking back unblinking, brave. I hoped I had the same look.

He'd thought about it, our father said, and concluded that he had a *right* to expect us, his sons, in the months to come, to also work *extremely* hard—in school—and to take care of our mother. It was important for *us* to know that *he* expected *us* to make *him,* Daddy, *proud.*

He shook a second cigarette from the package, tamped the mouthend, lit it, inhaled.

You three are going to Canada, he said softly; the words came out in smoke. He'd organized it all, he said. The day after tomorrow a plane would fly us to Singapore. There, we'd board a ship for Liverpool. And then, from England, on another ship, we'd sail to Canada.

Boom! That was it. The big news. It made me shiver. No discussion, no questions. A plane, a ship, another ship. Where the hell was Singapore? Where was Liverpool? Where England? Where Canada? They were just names. *Canada*—the land of

Grampa, Gramma, uncles, aunts, cousins, canoes, oranges, cow-boys, Indians, and now also honey and milk.

Two days later, when British soldiers hiding from the sun in a guard shack at Kemajoran Airport made no move to come out, my father impatiently ordered us driven straight onto the tarmac—Batavia needed him and the office Jeep back. The sharp smells of oil and hot metal hit us as the driver wheeled past long rows of black-green aircraft; in the distance planes quivered in the moist air. And then we came to one, a Dakota, that was ready and roaring, invisible propellors spinning, but boy, don't walk into one—minced meat! On the plane's shadow side we stepped onto soft asphalt where a line-up of civilians and luggage waited.

Our father's khaki shirt was stained with dark patches of sweat; he wore the sleeves rolled up to just below his armpits. One thing I'd learned from him for life was how to towel my back dry like a man. Until I saw him once in a communal bath-room in Tjimahi, I'd only seen women do it, just a gentle dab-bing. Holding the towel with both hands across his shoulders he had jerked it back and forth hard, then his middle back and rear end, until he turned lightly pink. In the airport heat his eyes were watering and he was squinting and breathing fast, so goodbyes were quick. He clasped Jerry's and my hands, gave us deep looks, and had to shout his take-care-of-your-mother instructions. His lips saying *meisje,* "little girl," he took our mother gently by the shoulders and kissed her on the mouth. Then he jumped back into the Jeep and it raced off, in seconds blurring in the haze. Jerry and my mother stared after it and I shoved our suitcases forward with my feet. Didn't they know by now? People always went away.

Jerry and I got window seats in the Dakota, him behind me, but for most of the four-hour flight to Singapore we flew inside cloud. Once it shredded and the earth below showed as brown snakes in dark dense grass. "Sumatra!" yelled Jerry, who knew geography. Next to me my mother leaned over to look—but we were pushing into cloud again. She didn't mind. "Another damn adventure, eh?" she said smiling. She half stood, turned, and over the engines' drone shouted it at Jerry, "Adventure!" Sitting again she watched the grey fleece whipping by my window for a while—her eyes thinking, far away.

Breakfast done, mother located, the day on board could begin. The first moment topside always blinded, but then the glare paled and what came into focus were the decks of that great gleaming marvellous ship already swarming with men in khaki. On the first day I'd been in a fever to check out all of her before nightfall. Jerry was, too, I think, and, after waving at strangers shrinking on the dock, we explored together for a while. But Jerry was more serious about it, had always loved ships, had drawn portholes on the walls of his bedroom on the plantation. So in the engine room, when I yelled that I couldn't stand the racket, that it made my teeth shake, he shrugged and went down the narrow oily stairs by himself. Back outside I waited a bit. Singapore seagulls still trailed us but already there was nothing, nothing to see but water; we were a cork. Then I set off alone and ran up and down decks, stairways, and corridors and in and out of crew quarters, cargo holds (where the soldiers and Jerry would sleep), mess halls, sick wards, galleys, stockrooms, laundries, and lounges. I kept at it long after dark—the ship was huge. On day two I made the same rounds, but by dinner was concentrating on lounges and, especially, decks.

And there they were then, lazing in the sun from bow to stern, several thousand glowing Jap-killers, winners of the war, many shirtless, shoeless, unshaven, many with bad teeth, many with fine moustaches, and all mine to pick and choose from. Not to make friends of—it was no use making friends—but to be with, to talk to. Listen to mostly: they liked to do the talking. So that's what I did; I roamed the decks, wading through soldiers, scouting, every day after breakfast, and after lunch and, unless there was a party in the lounges, after dinner. For more than three years I'd watched, listened to, and smelled women; on those bright decks it was men.

To get to slightly know all of them was the plan—except the bandaged ones or those in sick wards; that meant pain—so I skirted soldiers already met, even if they waved me over, and zeroed in on strangers. Making contact wasn't hard: I was the only kid by himself and perhaps I reminded them of a little brother, a nephew, a cousin, a son. I'd target a soldier for a small reason, long hands, freckles, and go and stand or sit by him, not too close, and wait. When he noticed me—and sooner or later he'd have to—I'd have my question ready. How I came up with it, I don't know, but I must have asked it a hundred times.

"Have you scars?"

A puzzled look.

"On the body?"

"Ah. I see. . . . Well. . . . Yes, here . . . ," and the soldier might hold out an arm or turn a calf or point to his neck. I'd touch the scar, trace it with a finger—connection made! Every man had scars, of course, in all shapes and each with a different feel. Scars, if not from battle, then from tramping through jungles or the sharp-edged grass, *alang-alang,* from falls and burns, from vermin bites, and even some boy-scars.

"How happen?" was the next question in my newly growing English, and then I'd shut up and listen. I was seldom prompted to speak. The few times I did start to say something, about my own scar from camp, for example, the eyes looking at me would turn uneasy. "Let me talk, please," the eyes said. A child's attention probably felt warm to men long unused to it, but attending to a child might be asking a little too much.

There was one soldier I approached about scars too hastily. He said nothing, never moved his slightly bulging blue eyes from the sea. He was a stocky man, balding, not tanned, wearing shorts and a khaki singlet. Always alone, he'd stand leaning at a railing, watching the waves, smoking. Other soldiers stopped by, said something, patted him on the back, but he stayed inside himself. At mealtimes he'd go below, return, and clump down again at sunset for the night. Dozens and dozens of little round scars and little round red and yellow wounds marked the tops of his hands and his thick pale arms. All day long he lit cigarettes, smoked them, then butted them on himself. No one would tell me why. "Be careful with us," was all a soldier with grey sideburns said to me once. So, I just listened.

"How happen?" though, was like opening a tap: every scar had a story and one story ran into another and, as my chosen man was usually in a group, the others would show off scars and tell more tales, top one another, boast, turn mishaps into adventures. Scar talk was fun but only lasted—the sessions had a sameness—until the men drifted back, briefly, to the war; not to the fighting, not to the enemy (I heard no Japanese hate stories on the ship), but to mates unforgotten, in snippets, ". . . liked to whistle, the bastard, even whistled pissing," ". . . the little bugger was too *young*." And then, as if they couldn't hold back any longer, they'd swirl around to what their minds really brimmed with—home, going bloody home! No stopping the flow then. Sprawled (no deckchairs for soldiers) by a railing for the breeze or, come the afternoon heat, inside a shadow, they'd rush on, each in his own dreamy or heated or sober way, about who and what was waiting at home as remembered in spun-out detail from months or years before—a woman, family, friends, a dog, a cat, a horse, a workplace, a pub, a bed like no other, the *richest* sounds and smells and tastes, streets or fields known in the dark, weather that was in the bones, on and on. And after a while the memories would slowly give way to hopes, to wishes, to plans—by which time, of course, I'd be fairly ignored. Each man wanted his say and being soldiers they weren't shy about horning in but, being fellow soldiers, they also knew when to be still. A hum of deep voices and laughs and smells of tobacco and sweat. Under the sun, cradled by waves, I listened and listened.

And didn't grasp very much, at first. It wasn't just that English was strange; it often sounded weirdly different from soldier to soldier. As I was talked to, or at, I often had to fake understanding for fear of the speaker losing interest. That wasn't difficult: in the camps I'd learned to wear a mask, to look all-ears while shutting off inside. But as I shammed interest on the decks I was also very alert and, slowly, new words sank in. My "mask," though, pretty well ruled out asking for explanations—and unknown English words piled up. What to do? The no-friendship distance I felt I had to keep probably also lost me those few who might have kindly helped. Jerry I seldom saw: he was with soldiers on some far-off deck, ate with them, slept with them in an airless hold in a hammock. My mother, the same: she was hardly ever alone, talking, laughing, feeling as free, I think, as a bird; I rarely disturbed her. So I never learned English faster than at a trickle.

I did search out my mother once about a word, and she was no help. I was hearing it constantly and then I heard it in regard to her. A sailor hosing down our deck grunted it at another sailor as she swept by on one of her walks. Minutes later I pinned her down in the smaller of the two reading lounges jam-packed with green-leather chairs and sofas and paintings of horsemen. She was settling in to play bridge with three officers, one of them her friend Cyril, a tall, stern-looking man with grey hair and a small grey moustache he nibbled at. Cyril, a major, sometimes joined my mother on her marches, slapping his leg with a swagger stick, and he'd given her a tiny book of poetry. In our bunks in the dark I'd asked about him. She answered that, when they were still almost strangers except that she knew he too was married, Cyril had coaxed her to guess his age. "Forty-six," she'd said, because of his hair. "Good God, no!" Cyril had laughed. "Thirty-two." What surprised her, she said, wasn't so much his age as his boyish laugh. Then they had become friends. *The Golden Treasury* fitted in her purse.

I liked Cyril: he made me a gift too. It was taking ages to learn English, but Cyril, out of the blue, taught me the gist of geography in minutes. We had never had much to say to each other, and wouldn't again, but one rough-weather afternoon in the crowded cocktail lounge he weaved over to where I was doing my daily check of the ship's course-chart. The miles-sailed line I understood, but nothing at all of the rest of the map. That was just one more "mystery." Since we had left camp, mysteries, aside from shocks, had sprung up from every direction and each one felt like a short rap on the head; some days I'd feel a bit stunned. In Camp Makasar I'd known *all* that was to be known about how to live in Makasar. But that kind of knowledge, clearly, wasn't enough any more, or even, it seemed, of much use. Every day I'd discover what I did *not* know, and what everybody else did and expected that I did, too, so that, as with the meaning of new English words, I'd feel uneasy about asking, and waited, and found out some other way. The list had swelled: movies, Johnny Walker, how the war was won, applesauce, rubbers, Popeye, adding, subtracting, dividing, cricket, Frank Sinatra, flying fish, atom bomb, spelling, Big Ben, chewing gum, Harry Truman, roller coaster, where water came from, *underwear*, jitterbugging, Stalin, Donald Duck, cocktail, the Depression, destroyer, Winnie, scarecrow, Benny Goodman, Eskimos, marmalade, garter belt, the U.N., radar, Tarzan, mistletoe, skyscraper, Napoleon, flame-thrower, toboggan, gangster, Piccadilly Circus, Nepal, Lana Turner. When I grouched about it, my mother would say cheerily not to worry—I'd had no school, after all; I'd go to school; I'd like school; I'd catch up in school. My father's word, school.

Now Cyril delivered his own little rap. Wide-legged on the pitching floor, he loomed over me and poked his leather stick at the chart's top right-hand corner, at a "cross" with its tips marked W, N, E, and S.

West, North, East, and South, right? he asked.

Masked at once, I nodded. The words did sound like the Dutch *West, Noord, Oost, Zuid,* but those had no meaning either.

All right, Cyril said, the ship's next stop was Rangoon. He put a forefinger on Rangoon on the map and stretched his thumb down to Singapore—Rangoon was north of Singapore, right? Or—Singapore lay south of Rangoon, right?

I nodded firmly, yes, of course, but I could feel Cyril giving me a look.

Telling me to wait right there, he suddenly lurched out of the lounge.

Fine. I liked being in the bar. The *Devonshire* was "dry" but even so people in there often smelled nicely of whisky or gin— and then they always enjoyed treating. At the ship's big Christmas party, where hairy soldiers danced in women's clothes and my mother made me sing a Dutch sailors' ditty, I was stood to fourteen tomato juices.

But Cyril was back in just moments, carrying in front of him a ball of many colours mounted at a slant inside a hoop. He placed the thing, slightly larger than a soccer ball, at the centre of the tilting chart table, and set it spinning. That, he said gravely, was the world. It was called a "globe," and looked exactly like the real world as seen from—if I could *imagine* it—extremely high up in the sky. Well, *yes, I could*! The moon hung about here, his stick showed, the sun there, and the stars, well, everywhere. He tapped the globe's white top and bottom: North Pole, South Pole. North and South, right? East and West were easy: I should just remember that the sun rose East, went down West. He fixed on Rangoon and Singapore again. North–South, South–North, right? East of Singapore was—Borneo. West—Sumatra, right? He asked me to name some countries, located them, and from each country his stick tracked always back to Singapore. We found Indonesia (a mass of islands), Japan (just a few), Holland (tiny: my father was right), England (small), Germany (also small), Canada (big), Russia (the biggest). I could've come up with two or three more, but Cyril thought that was enough. I had now seen the world, he said, so I could never get lost. Then he swayed away clutching the globe which I didn't see again on the ship; didn't need to: I knew geography now.

At the card table, my mother had put her cards down and, eyebrows up in question, smiled at me. I said politely "Excuse me" to the men and then asked her quietly, *"Wat betekent* 'fucking'?" Her smile faded a little. Unsure, she told me to say the word again. "Fucking," I said, also to the three men staring very hard at their cards. My mother thought a moment, sighed, shook her head, and said, no, *liefje,* "little love," sorry, she didn't know it, and took up her cards again. But did she really not know? Yes. Jerry and I would learn in time that three or four words in both English and Dutch just passed by her, apparently meaningless. We could say them anytime.

Still, I *had* to know—if only because it was the most-used word on board. Fuck this. Fuck that. Fuck off. Fuck you. Fuck *me.* Fuck the army. I'm fucked. What the fuck? I don't give a fuck. Don't fuck around. The fuck you say? You know fuck-all. That fucker is a real fuck. He's an okay fuck. Well, fuck me gently. Where's me fucking tea? How the fuck should I know? I fucking love her. I love fucking her. That'll fuck you up. By no fucking means. Jesus fucking Christ. It's so fucking hot you can fucking fry fucking eggs on the fucking deck. What the sailor had said about my mother was: "Now *that's* a fucking lady." Certainly there was no word as rich in Dutch. I didn't ask anyone else about it again; listening on the decks was how I got the hang of it.

What a school, the decks. Non-stop, through the long bright days and soft evenings, I learned about English and about mysteries. Everything said or shown, if understood even a little, I shovelled into my head—soak it up, wolf it down; sort later. Climbing into my bunk at night I'd be so gorged I could hardly talk. Yet, that was the best time for talk, for questions—if, of course, my mother was still awake. The hours on the ship were certainly the longest, and greediest, I'd ever lived, and maybe they were for her, too. One night she was still reading, luckily, because I needed to get something off my chest.

Were eyes important, I asked, my own eyes closed, seeing the evening again.

Below, she finished her sentence, put the book down, switched off her reading light.

Yes, she said in the dark. Very.

Why?

To see with, of course, but also because eyes could tell you something about people. Eyes could be *read* a little.

The cabin hummed, creaked, and outside the half-open porthole the sea hissed.

Could they always be read?

Not always, no.

I knew that, I said. Wandering around Singapore one afternoon, I told her, Jerry and I had suddenly come across a dozen Japanese soldiers digging up a street; their young British guard sat on a rock reading a magazine. Jerry and I stood very still. I hadn't seen a Japanese in three months. The prisoners fixedly hacked away with pickaxes, shirts wet, not looking up. Then one did, stretching, and for a moment his black eyes held us— unreadable. Standing straight, legs wide, he had looked as dangerous as ever and everything in me had cried *Bow!* Then he bent to work again. Jerry and I ran back to the Seaview Hotel, up to room 48, flopped on our beds, and I, anyhow, promptly fell asleep.

I'd told her the story before, she said. I should forget about Japanese eyes.

Had she noticed, I asked, that some men on board had really deep eyes?

Deep?

With more *in* them.

Well, yes. Some soldiers had seen a lot.

What?

Pain and killing. Death.

They'd all seen that.

Yes, but—think about it—maybe some soldiers had been shaken up more by the things they'd seen. Maybe they still felt hurt by it.

I wouldn't mind deep eyes myself, I said.

That would be nice.

Could *she* read eyes?

A little, she hoped. But eyes really just gave a feeling about someone. You could often trust the feeling, but eyes could also shut you out on purpose, or lie. People were hard to understand, even a little, and that was the truth. Inside they were, well, mysteries.

Her word, too! I said I had a story to tell her.

Please. She was half-asleep.

After dinner I'd gone out on deck, I began, and sat down near a group of soldiers where one was playing a harmonica. Did she remember *my* harmonica?

She yawned. Yes.

Keep it short, I thought. The soldiers had sung songs, I went on, and so had I. Then they danced. . . .

How nice, she whispered. I heard her sigh and turn.

I stopped talking and lay open-eyed in the darkness. The harmonica man had first played soldier songs like "It's a Long Way to Tipperary," "Pack Up Your Troubles," "For Me and My Gal"—heard endlessly on the decks after nightfall, some men singing softly, some bellowing; on black nights just glowing cigarettes showed and the smell of the men and of salt seemed stronger. This was a starry night, warm and windless, with the ship rolling, but smoothly. Other soldiers wandered over and joined the singing. Men pulled at small bottles on the sly, handed them on. I was offered cigarettes on the decks, and usually accepted, but strong drink never. Then the harmonica player switched to jazz. There was finger-snapping, whistling, and several men grabbed a mate and started dancing, stand-up wrestling really, with each wanting to lead. As happened often, it got a bit rowdy. Dancers kicked other dancers not hard in the rear, tried to trip them—easy on the tilting deck—chased each other whooping. One soldier fell, dragged his "pardner" along, and from below the two lunged at legs to drop others. Men became boys, big boys. I enjoyed it a lot. Sitting on the still-warm deck I laughed out loud and for once squished to death the always hovering "It-never-lasts" thought.

The music maker took a break, but the men didn't; rough play went on and, as I'd hoped, it gradually shifted into the "push game." It was my favourite, better than table-tennis, tag, cards, shuffle-board, anything. Men formed a tight, not large circle around a man singled out for some reason; no one ever volunteered. Centre-man could break free only by ramming a circle-man out or yanking one in—and then that spot was his. The circle had to stay round and fixed, but circle-men could help each other and some of them, it's true, liked to bully a little. If the centre-man went for a "weak link," the link and his neighbours could push him off hard—no hitting—hurling him to where hands waited to shove him sideways to be thrust away again, on and on, so that he floundered faster and faster back and forth and around the circle. After a minute or two even a big strong centre-man would have to retreat to safety, the circle's dead-centre, and, breathing hard, sweating, rest until yelled taunts made him rush in for more punishment. Those who fought on and broke through were usually wiry men fast on their feet. Giving up was a way out for a tired centre-man, though he mightn't be let go right away; the game wasn't always played entirely in fun.

I'd been a centre a few times, never a circle-man—too small—and I was asked again that night. "C'mon kid!" Wonderful. Inside the ring I danced, skipped, and spun away from the big hands—once caught, I'd be just a rag doll, legs dangling, tossed unhurt from man to man. Speed was the thing, darts, turns, fake lunges. Be a water spider, a spirit. But the circle-men, I could tell, began to grow restless with my dodging; they'd also been at it for a while. I'd escaped before by slithering through a man's legs . . . and it was time. I dove forward onto the deck between a wide-spread set of legs and was almost through when the legs slammed together. Men laughed. Me, too: I'd come close.

The hands hoisting me up felt strong—a tall soldier, lean, black hair matted to his forehead, smiling. "And now, little man …," he said softly, and then he bent and put his left arm behind my knees, the right around my shoulders, and, straightening, heaved me from the deck and carried me in front of him towards the railing. We're wrestling, I thought. But he took another step, and then he was holding me out above the sea. "Hey!" "Hey Jack!" I heard voices. He didn't lean on the railing for support, just stood there stiff against the roll of the ship, weighted arms straight ahead. He had a grip on my right knee and shoulder, but I could feel a tremble in his arms. *Don't squirm!* yelled my body. As the ship listed our way, the faint sizzle of it cutting through the sea below rose up fast to a roar—and in the corner of my eye foaming dark water raced up, so close. Then the ship tilted back and the water yawed out of sight. *Don't scream!* His face was a foot away, wet, and he was panting, his mouth turned down. Eyes as black as his hair and blinking very fast looked past me into the night. I heard voices again, murmuring, humming almost. "Don't *touch* him," was said clearly. The strain in his arms eased when he crooked them a little. As the ship sloped our way again he swung around on his heels in one jerk and gently stood me up on the deck.

A yard or so away, many wide-eyed men were bunched around us. No one spoke and in that second I ducked my head and charged into them and they made room fast. I ran for our deck, our cabin, my mother, but decided no, and, looping widely around, ran to the cave instead. In that safe place, after a while, the shaking stopped. What happened? Why? *"Be careful with us!"* What had I done? Already the moments were turning dreamlike. Had I ever been that scared before? Yes . . . I saw them again—the smile-shaped lips of Lieutenant Tanaka, the still, black eyes on my mother's bowed head. . . . No one asked about the Jack incident in the days to follow. I didn't see him again but I never forgot his eyes.

I thought less often of leaping overboard after that. I was still tempted in harbours, though, to swan dive into the brown oily water, especially because we weren't allowed ashore in Rangoon, Bombay, Karachi, Aden, and Port Said. I would've swum amongst pitching little rowboats from which shouting men threw up rope loops with baskets to sell us fruit, cloth, hats, carvings, and amongst screaming brown boys who dove like fish—what a life!—after tossed coins. Sure, in Aden, we were given more Red Cross clothes, underwear *again*, warm shirts, pyjamas, real shoes; and in Port Said the "cheep-cheep man" came aboard, an amazing Egyptian magician who smelled of pineapple and whose closing trick was—twice more I'd see him on ships' decks—suddenly releasing dozens of fluttering, cheeping chicks out of children's ears, their shirts, his own ears, his *mouth,* and from beneath his greasy robes and fez. But only in Colombo (Sri Lanka) did they let us off.

A purple, smoking bus took in interested civilians at the dock and drove us to a swimming hole up in the hills above the city. White flowers drifted on the pond with round leaves the size of car wheels. The musty-smelling water lay like glass in the shadow of a many-trunked banyan tree from one of whose branches hung a rope with a cross-bar at the end. Taking turns, we climbed high up the worn-smooth trunk holding the bar, then jumped, and swung out yelling, stomach heaving, in a great arc over the pond to let go midway on the return swing and plunge down like a cannonball. The water tasted like old tea but the "flying" lodged forever in dreams. One of the young English mothers, a blonde, vaulted into the pond with her son around her neck and, clambering out, beige bathing-suit clinging nicely, said it made her feel like Tarzan. Tarzan? As we wheeled back down to Colombo, she told me what she knew of him. In the ship's library I found *Tarzan of the Apes* and *Jungle Tales of Tarzan.* I couldn't read the books then, but they had pictures. Tarzan was an eye-opener—pure, strong, brave, and a fine swimmer—just the man I needed. If only I'd known him in the camps! A master spirit, he promptly moved in.

That night there was a party, of course. Parties marked steaming into ports and out again, crossing the Equator, Christmas, New Year's, Saturday nights, and "special occasions." Maybe the passengers on that ship felt every new day was reason to celebrate. The little bottles showed up then; in the bar, crew members played saxophone, piano, bass, and drums. It was fun on the decks, but more fun in the lounges. Soldiers dressed up the once, for Christmas; officers came to every party starched and gleaming. But for me the lounges won out mostly because of women, perfumed, rouged, shiny-haired women in cool thin dresses and high heels. Women who held cigarettes and stemmed glasses in small hands, who smiled, who laughed softly, who nimbly observed all the faces around them, and beyond, and whose bodies moved like lazy water. And because of women, there was dancing.

Lounge parties were for adults only, except at Christmas, so I had to spy through on-deck portholes—I watched mime, really, as sea and wind drowned sound. Stewards slid the doors between the reading lounges and bar into walls, making one big room, lowered lights, and cleared the darkest corner for dancing. My mother attended some parties and seldom stayed late; she'd sip at whisky and ginger ale, unhandily smoke a few cigarettes, and when she danced, she did so just as she sang, out of sync, though not awkwardly, and thoroughly enjoyed herself. I watched all the parties, I think, and quit when the musicians did. The dances had a sameness: quiet and polite at first, though everyone knew each other; then, as dancing started, warming up, and working onward to very warm, especially if the ship was tossing a little. Around nine, the men gathered around the bar, the thirty or thirty-five women, many of them mothers, scattered themselves around in two- and three-somes with stewards scurrying to fetch white lemonade in fluty glasses; the hard drink came later. Men crowded one another at the bar, slapped shoulders, laughed hard, and slinked looks at the women who, at that point, never glanced their way. It was a pity, though, there were so few women. A lot of men didn't dance, just sat or stood about, glass in hand, and grew red-faced and less steady; some would end up arm-wrestling, like boys. The women never slipped back to being girls.

On New Year's Eve, at the last second of 1945, the ship let off several long lonely honks (maybe heard in Libya or in Greece), sounded whistles, bells, a siren. In the lounges, men and women ran around kissing one another, tossing pink paper ribbons, blowing gold paper trumpets (my mother's lay on my bunk later), touching glasses, and then, linking arms, swaying, some crying, singing. The strains of "Auld Lang Syne" reached me at my post, nose pushed against the porthole. I was, though, mostly watching an officer and a woman in the dance corner, the only ones left. Already holding each other, they kissed the midnight kiss, but then, turning slowly as if still dancing, they didn't stop. Pressing closer, they kissed on. Kissing, they wrapped both arms around the other, her hands settling way down his spine. Like one body they were, kissing the longest kiss. They kissed through all the commotion, were still kissing when dance music must have started up because several couples joined them. Others then began to wander outdoors to cool off: my cue to slip away, but I couldn't. As if alone, the two went on kissing—and then I saw her hands moving on his back, oh, moving only a little, up and down, up and down.

"Enjoying yourself?" asked my mother. I whirled around. There she stood smiling, flushed, Cyril alongside, smiling, too. Startled, I nodded yes. "Happy New Year, *liefje*," she said, her eyes hugging me, taking me in, Hubie's boots, short pants . . . and stopping. She leaned forward quickly and so blocked out Cyril, and whispered in Dutch, "Is that *you*?" Then she turned, clasped Cyril's elbow, and they marched off. I looked down and saw a definite swell.

Even as nights grew chilly, even as we turned right, just after Gibraltar, up into the cold Atlantic, I stood my watch at the round windows. On party nights something lovely happened there in the half-dark where earrings flashed. I saw it the first night out of Singapore and it was just as fine to see a month later on the night before docking in Liverpool. Every party again, watching, I'd feel myself melting inside. Gazing at those men and women dancing together I'd begin to feel warm and easy and so happy. Holding one another lightly, chests and bellies seldom touching, they stepped and dipped and spun for joy.

THREE / DPs, Brides, and Other Aliens

THE COLOUR WAS GREY, all the shades of grey. Sky, clouds, rain, river, trees, streets, shops, houses, cars, and Londoners came in grey. If the wind had a colour it would have been grey. There was also some red: double-decker buses, blood puddles in Madame Tussaud's Chamber of Horrors, and the nails of Red Cross women. That was London, when I looked at it inside my mind, grey with bits of red so you wouldn't go crazy. For two months we were stuck there in fog and drizzle amidst burned-out ruins and cripples in military overcoats, and we shouldn't have been.

In chilly Liverpool, civilians had disembarked first. It was late afternoon and raining. Wind tugged at the gangplank and far beneath our feet black water churned in the crack between the ship and the dock. On the wharf, behind a double line-up of trucks, a crowd jostled under black umbrellas, singing and cheering. A welcome for the soldiers—who in their hundreds pressed against railings deck upon deck high above, but few of whom cheered back. Once on land, I meant to turn and wave up at them, but no, an unsmiling pale-faced woman drew my mother under her umbrella, "Come along, Mrs. Hillen." She hurried us away, just us three, a good distance along the curving wharf, out of sight of the ship, into a round-roofed shed with open wide doors. It was dry there but no warmer. Footsteps echoed on the stone floor; further inside a single light burned over a black steel door. The woman told Jerry and me to sit on metal chairs by the entrance and wait with our luggage. She promised tea. "Papers," she said to us as explanation opening the black door for my mother; it clanged shut behind them. Jerry took a book out of his suitcase.

Outside the doors, the darkening wharf showed clusters of deserted cranes, rain spattering, but no people, no trucks. I couldn't even hear the *Devonshire*, but they must have started unloading the soldiers by then and carting them off the other way. I could have "floated" over for a last look, but I didn't. I was just very sorry I hadn't waved. I should've waved. I should've had time to wave to the soldiers, many probably a little drunk and so quiet, perhaps, because they really had come home alive. I had no friends up there, but waving was a way of saying goodbye: I hadn't said goodbye. And the last days had been among the best, too. All the way up the Atlantic that great ship had fought whipping rain and, in the Bay of Biscay, a terrific storm—which had even some of the toughest soldiers puking. The wondrous light from the decks had glowed *inside* of her then where, cozy and safe but cooped up, men had drunk more from the small bottles, sung more, bought more tomato juices. To be inside her still, the little gong ringing for dinner. . . .

I'd never before been so cold as in those first minutes in England. We wore our best "warm clothes" from the Aden hand-outs: pale-grey flannel suits with short pants and little grey, what our mother called, "proper English-schoolboy" caps. No overcoats. In the silent shed Jerry's knees looked blueish, but he was reading so he probably didn't notice. Reading, he would "disappear," which could be irritating. Jerry had already spoken a little English when we boarded and then picked it up fast; he had an excellent brain, people said. We'd both spent our days with the soldiers, but he was an English-speaking fifteen-year-old, a man almost; had he begun to feel the age gap on the ship? Before, on the plantation, in the camps, in Tjimahi, in Batavia, in Singapore, it had always been just him and me. Before, except when they'd wrested him away in camp, I'd always told him whatever was on my mind—not to tell him felt almost like lying—and I'd always had his close attention. On the ship, though, I hadn't needed him much; I'd hardly seen him. And so, on the ship, Jerry might have grown busier with Jerry.

I missed the ship, I said loudly, watching my breath.

He nodded, but read on in the thin light—in the old days, he would've put his book down.

Should we just climb the hell back in her and hide?

He shut the book. No, that wasn't a good idea. Better wait for Mom.

Didn't *he* miss the ship?

He hesitated. Sure.

England was bloody awful.

We'd been in England ten minutes.

Bloody fucking awful.

We should give it a chance.

Well, when the hell were we going to Canada?

Very soon.

Where was our tea?

It hadn't come yet.

I was definitely not staying in England.

It wouldn't be for long.

I had to get to Canada. Fast.

He did, too, yes.

On and on, we kept it up. Finally he held up his book, an English book—Jerry had learned to *read* English in the month at sea. Should he read to me? Like he used to?

No thanks.

Twinges of homesickness for the ship had started. Long ago I'd been homesick once or twice, and the stomach-cramp sadness always brimmed at dusk.

About an hour later—no tea—our mother and the woman returned. A car was on the way, the woman said. We looked at our mother: lips pressed together, a bad sign, she shook her head no—don't ask questions. There was a soldier behind the wheel of the black car. The woman helped pile the luggage and us in the back on a wide leather seat and, opposite it, on two fold-down small ones. She did try to smile then, and said, "Good luck, Mrs. Hillen." We drove down the wharf, away from the *Devonshire*; our thin-lipped mother, staring into the dark outside, told us she had to think—don't talk.

Somewhere deep in Liverpool, the soldier dropped us off at a tall house that showed no lights, where an old woman with a single thick white pigtail let us in. She shuffled ahead down a narrow dark hall to a room with three cots jammed together, a window painted black, pink-and-brown striped walls, and a lightbulb in a knot of wires on the ceiling. The cots, on which we set down our luggage, had bare mattresses, pillows, and, at the foot of each, a folded grey blanket. "Follow me, dearies," said the woman. She switched off the light, and we moved down another unlit hall towards an open door at the end. In that room, a twin of the first but with a table and chairs, she served us plates of boiled potatoes, carrots, mutton, and mugs of tea. "Good night, dearies," she said then, and shut the door behind her. Not a sound in that house, and we ate without speaking.

Jerry liked all food, but he and I had never had mutton before. He jabbed the meat with his fork and said, "I hate this," but emptied his plate of course.

Our first night in England—mutton, a bathroom Jerry couldn't find when he got sick, stone-cold beds, our mother's distress. The mattresses, pillows, and blankets felt damp and we didn't undress; over the blankets we spread our own dry towels. At last, lying between us in the dark, our mother began to whisper—a little trembly, from the cold probably. In the shed, she said, she'd talked about "papers" to a man. He'd sat behind a big steel desk, smoked a pipe, and she guessed he wasn't thirty yet. He'd fiddled with the pipe, had even unscrewed the mouthpiece and blown black spit out of it. Every time he spoke he'd first take a puff, hold in the smoke, then, speaking, watch it cross-eyed trailing out of his mouth—"I could've hit him!" Oh yes, he'd said, he entirely believed her story about the British authorities in Batavia saying because she was born in Canada she was a British subject, and her sons too, and so the British government was responsible for repatriating her to Canada. But Madam, he'd said, Batavia was *wrong*. Madam had married a Dutchman. Madam, therefore, was *Dutch,* and so were her sons. That was the law. Madam and her sons were the responsibility of the *Dutch* government. It could repatriate them to The Netherlands. But in Batavia, she'd argued, *British* officials had posivitively said she was a *British* subject. Why fly us to Singapore otherwise? Put us up in a hotel for ten days? Pay our passage to Liverpool? Yes, he'd answered, it certainly was a grave error Batavia had made. Well, our mother had said, she and her boys had been prisoners of the Japanese for three and a half years. She hadn't been home for sixteen years. She wanted to go to Canada, and the *British* government in Batavia had promised to deliver her. She was halfway there. How about the other half? His government had *promised* it.

The man had put his damn pipe down then, leaned across the desk and, speaking slowly and coldly, had said: "Madam, you are not a British subject. You are an *alien*."

What was an alien? Jerry asked. I, to be honest, hadn't entirely followed her. Anyhow, hadn't our father arranged everything?

It meant, she said, that she didn't belong where she was. It meant that she was a foreigner, an outsider, a stranger. She was quiet a moment. It meant, she said, that she, no, that *we* were what they called Displaced Persons or DPs. Well, she knew about DPs all right. On the ship she'd heard there were hundreds of thousands, *millions*, of DPs all over the world—because of the war, because of prison camps. People with no country, no papers, no money, helpless, lost. Again she paused. Then she said out loud: "I'm no goddamn DP! I'm a goddamn Canadian! And you're no goddamn DPs, because you're mine!" Well, she'd used her strongest swear word. Whispering again, she told us to go to sleep. First thing tomorrow, you bet, we'd be taking the train for London. She didn't know how long it would take, but boys, we were going to Canada, we *were*, don't worry. Jerry did worry, I'm sure, but I didn't: she'd fix it okay. To me, as I drifted off, "DP" didn't sound so bad, sort of punchy—"Hello, I'm a DP!"

There was money on the streets of London. The Red Cross had put us up at the "Home for British Brides" at 80 Brooke Street, a four-storey, tiny-windowed house crusted with soot. Inside it was a tangle of murky corridors and creaking stairs never free of smells—fried fish, carbolic soap. Our windowless slant-walled attic room held two big beds, which filled the space as the cots had in Liverpool, and also a three-drawer dresser, a table lamp, and a washstand with bowl and pitcher; there were sheets and two blankets on each of the beds, and spares in the dresser. Some heat rose from below, enough so it wasn't very damp or cold; the toilet was just beneath on the fourth floor. We were extremely pleased: it was a nice room, and also private; the rest of the attic lay in dusty shadow. After we put down the luggage, Jerry and I were shooed out, and, it's true, we weren't in the fresh air a minute when Jerry found the sixpence—right there on a busy sidewalk in the middle of London. We bought fried potatoes, "chips," with vinegar and salt in a cone of news-paper, then wandered on, street in, street out, scanning for more money. That's what we did the first few days, roam around the hostel in widening circles, heads down, but the sixpence was it.

As she'd done all through the camps, our mother at once made our new space in the London attic "home." She switched the dresser and washstand around, pinned magazine pictures to the brownish yellow walls, draped a scarf around the dresser's mirror, and strung up a sheet between the beds so we had two bedrooms, with hers also serving as "living room." In time, a jar with pine twigs stuck in it, even flowers once or twice, would deck out the washstand. Overnight, she also somehow squelched her Liverpool let-down—just swallowed it—and from day one began phoning, writing letters, and visiting offices around the city to get us to Canada. She doggedly kept at it for the next two months. I'd seen drawings of Winston Churchill—the man who beat Hitler—as a fat, stubborn bulldog. Our mother was a slim bulldog. Did all DPs have to be bulldogs? She wasn't really as badly off as many because, of course, she could always ask to be shipped to Holland. But no, that was out of the question. Holland was in ruins itself. No, as long ago as the English conversations with our father, she'd made up her mind—she was going home to Canada "come hell or high water, period."

She used the hostel's phone in the ground-floor parlour, wrote letters on her bed, and walked to appointments; there was no money for buses. On the *Devonshire*, the Red Cross had given her a pound a week for each of us and they did so again in London. She was miserly with the money: treats were rare even though hostel food (after the ship's) was camp-blah because of rationing and endless boiling. The second week in London the Red Cross gave us more clothes, sweaters, overcoats. She needed shoes—the Aden shoes hurt her narrow long feet—but the Red Cross didn't have her size. What some of the hoarded money did go on, though, was a present each for Jerry and me, things we could choose ourselves, because, she said, as she had in Singapore, we "deserved" them. She didn't buy shoes for herself, so walked the streets in pain and, when out after dark, carried them and trod on in stocking feet. She bought, instead, a hat. She went on and on to us about hats; "A hat makes the woman," she claimed. The three of us finally bought the thing on Oxford Street, an expensive dashing chocolate-brown felt fedora. Very smart.

But maybe she knew what she was doing. She argued to go to Canada in the offices of the International Red Cross, the Canadian Red Cross, Canada House, and who knows where else. Jerry and I went along a few times and, before the hat, watched her going at it armed with just patience and smiles— and losing. The men and women behind desks were as unmovable as the pipe-smoker in Liverpool: she was not a British subject, therefore . . . And then one day—wearing the hat—she moved the heart of Colonel Quarles van Ufford, a Dutch repatriation officer. We never met him, but the colonel kindly phoned people, wrote people, and then he made a plan. My mother should at once cable her father, Grampa Watson in Toronto.

But that was several weeks away. Jerry and I by then had bought our presents. Jerry's choice was a black three-light flashlight like the silver one I got in Singapore (and lost at sea). Mine, well, I'd known what I wanted—even *more* than Hubie's soldier-on-a-horse—while still on board ship. On our rambles around London, every time I saw a swagger stick I yearned for one but also, because I'd seen them first on the *Devonshire*, I'd think of the ship, of her light, of tomato juice, of not waving to the soldiers, and feel the cramps stir. One rainy afternoon on the streets I asked Jerry again if he didn't still miss her.

A little, sure. The food was good.

A little? I'd give anything to be back inside her.

No, he didn't feel that strongly.

Why not? I'd never been so happy.

He hadn't always had a good time.

How could he not have a good time on the ship?

For one thing, he'd been bored often. And also, he'd been on his own.

I'd missed him and Mom, too, sometimes.

Yes, but we'd at least shared the cabin. In his hammock in the hold . . . nothing but men, like camp. The heat down there, and the stink—worse than camp. And the noise—all night long, snoring, sleep-talking, sleep-*screaming*. He'd often spent the night on deck.

In a narrow street we stopped under a shop's awning where runs of droplets curtained us in. And there, looking out from the shop's window were our twins—fists in their short-pants pockets (no overcoats), faces wet, silly caps pulled low. Jerry's twin stared down at his shoes; mine was watching me.

But hadn't his friend Bill often come out on deck with him? Hadn't they watched the stars?

I'd met Bill, a cheerful, rowdy, red-haired soldier. He liked to tell a joke and then laugh hard as if he, too, were hearing it for the first time.

Yes, Jerry said.

So he'd made a friend on board.

Several.

He'd been given the Gurkha knife.

Yes.

I envied him that short bent sword, a present from another soldier friend. Gurkhas were feared warriors from someplace called Nepal who soldiered for the British. The story was that when a Gurkha threw his favoured weapon at an enemy standing, say, ten yards away in high grass, the spinning knife would mow an ankle-high path and slice the man's Achilles tendons. Then the Gurkha would approach the fallen enemy. . . .

So he had friends, I insisted, a Gurkha knife—how could he not miss the ship?

I wouldn't understand, Jerry said, lifting our mother's soft eyes to my twin. He'd been lonely.

Braving the rain again, we walked on.

As for swagger sticks: French, Dutch, Canadian, and American military men didn't carry them, only British officers. They stuck out from armpits or slapped owners' legs as Cyril's had done—what finer thing, really, could you own? Bleak London had stores full of them. There was a "stick palace" near the hostel. Inside, it smelled of wet wool; dim yellow light revealed every type of umbrella, cane, baton, crutch, staff, swagger stick, walking stick, even sticks with knives or swords hidden inside, hanging from the ceiling, mounted on walls, crowding counters, and standing bunched in urns. Rejecting leather and bamboo, I finally chose a stick of some supple wood with a carved collie's head as a handle that just fitted my palm. I was perfectly pleased. I owned two things: the soldier on horseback and the stick, and the stick had no past. Jerry and my mother approved. Strangers said, "Nice stick!"

I ate and slept with it and on the toilet whacked the floor with it. Out on London's sidewalks, where I fell more and more into measuring buildings, rooftops, and trees (until it was routine) for imaginary Tarzan swing-travels, the stick acted as Tarzan's longish knife. It came along everywhere. To a concert in the Royal Albert Hall, for example, for which our mother was given tickets, perhaps by the colonel. Our parents had always listened to classical music with closed eyes; and sure, you did hear it fine then, could even *go away* inside it. The concert with full orchestra and perfumed air was Jerry's and my first and the mistake we made was not shutting our eyes—but we'd never seen a conductor before. A tall thin man in black, he led with his baton but also with flailing arms, flying hair, knee-bends, and wild little jumps. We caught each other's eyes then—the second mistake. And the third was for me to start conducting with my stick in my lap. If you try not to laugh, it'll come out in snorts. Suddenly our mother yanked the stick away and sat down on it.

The stick saw a lot of London because Jerry and I didn't like hanging around the hostel. The brides often seemed a little sad, a little lost, and their eyes might show pain. We'd lived for a long time, though, with anxious women, and couldn't get out on the wet streets fast enough. We were on our own, usually, because our mother, besides her reach-Canada errands, had volunteered for hostel chores, cleaning, doing washes, helping brides with letters and "papers." She was the oldest of the guests, most of whom were very young and often pregnant or already mothers. They must have wondered about her—the ritzy hat, *which* war she was a bride from. Still, she was the most experienced "bride" in that hive of babies and swollen women, and she knew about Canada. In the tatty little parlour and at the communal meals, she made friends with the women, many of whose mouths showed brown teeth—too much tea?—and who, like most people in sunless England, had pale faces.

Letters from grooms, above all, were what the brides craved: they were waiting for passage, after all, to a far-away land to join men they often hardly knew. Many of the soldier-grooms already back in Canada were, it seemed, "lazy" about writing or perhaps they didn't know how to either. Every morning, mail delivery set the hostel's mood. Afterwards, hands pressed into lower backs, women in housecoats restlessly wandered the halls, had sudden crying spells, screaming matches, sat on toilets moaning. Our mother invented groom-excuses then, and talked courage. What else to do? We heard her and it came down to this: Weren't they, the brides, lucky? What an adventure! Canada was beautiful, *so* beautiful, and big, no, *enormous*—and it was *because* of all that space, *because* of all those forests, fields, rivers, lakes, prairies, mountains, and seashores, that, honestly, every dream could be made true. Cities had wide clean streets, fine homes, lots of shops, cinemas, churches, parks. Farms had good land and fieldstone houses. Trains reached everywhere. And Canadians, well, Canadians were generous, reliable, hard-working, honest, funny, and gentle. And somewhere in there she'd make a strange little joke which even so always got a giggle: "I tell you—too *late*, of course—never marry a foreigner. I did and never will again!" She came to be trusted so well that women confided courtship claims to her which, she'd hear later, turned out to be just heartbreaking lies. Some brides arrived in Canada only to find other wives already in place, even with children; and "farm owners" turned out to be farmhands; "engineers," labourers; "factory directors," clerks; "landlords," janitors; "big homes," shacks. Joan, a small woman from Scotland, round with child, showed everyone in an atlas the wide brown streak that runs from Mexico to Alaska. The Canadian portion of the Rocky Mountains, her man had told her in their early cuddling days, was owned by his well-to-do family.

And the stick also saw a lot of London on outings with young Red Cross women, Canadians, many of them, with fine white teeth. Maybe they felt sorry for Jerry and me but, on their free days, pairs of them now and then took us out for the afternoon; trips, I think, that might've been a little bit for themselves, too. In a double-decker bus, the Underground, or a taxi, with the women mostly talking to each other, we'd cross the city, visit a museum, a church, a famous home, a park, and afterwards often the bar of some private club where they'd meet men friends. On the way home we enjoyed listening to how the men rated.

I liked it when our keepers strolled a little ahead, swaying nicely in high heels, stocking seams climbing into the warmth of their skirts, wrinkles in stockings smoothed with wetted, red-nailed fingertips. The women were forgotten, though, in Madame Tussaud's Waxworks Museum. We thought it, or at least I did, London's finest attraction. Twice we visited, and the second time some of the eerily lifelike notables, many of whom Jerry knew about, were almost like friends; you wanted to say hello. Especially to short Joseph Stalin. A monster, I'd heard, a killer of millions, but there was something, well, grandfatherly about him. For several years, seeing him in newsreels, I'd feel that, if only he and I had a chance to talk, he'd nod and smile, and stop it.

For us, though, and for many, to tell by the crowds, the core of Tussaud's was the downstairs Chamber of Horrors with its murderers and murdered and amazing tortures invented to hurt or madden. The bodies and faces twisted in agony and all the blood had adult visitors gasping, not lingering. What bothered me both afternoons were not the gruesome displays but that, looking at them, I felt an old "coldness." When the Japanese had knocked women around, I'd wanted to turn away, but couldn't—my neck was in some grip and my feet seemed nailed down, and I'd sweated and watched. In the first weeks in camp, I'd walked away from beatings trembling, bewildered, but later I'd felt nothing, really; it was so routine. Now it was the same thing with the pain and cruelty on show at Tussaud's: I was fascinated and unmoved. One of the Red Cross women told us about a man who'd bet that after lights-out he could stay all night alone in the Chamber of Horrors. At some point he'd leaned against a wall for a smoke, but when he bent to butt the cigarette under his shoe, his heart stopped. Next morning he was found held upright by a nail in the wall caught in the collar of his coat. I wouldn't be scared to stay over by myself, I boasted to Jerry—and maybe I really wouldn't have been. And then, a few evenings later, a blonde pregnant London bride came running in off the street with her face bloodied. She'd had a set-to with her former "fellow." For a while in the parlour I watched other brides stroking her, bathing her face, crying along. Then I trudged up to our attic, and didn't even bother mentioning it.

That weekend, though, there was a different sort of outing. Another set of women fetched us in a taxi about noon, and we drove a short way to an officers' club. First lunch, they promised, then a movie. What movie? They didn't know. Through the dining room's high, wide windows daylight poured onto white-clothed tables of cheery men and women in uniform; Jerry and I were the only kids. Each table carried a little vase of flowers and bottles of wine and, as lunch went on, people laughed more, drank toasts. It was an eating party. Maybe it was a holiday. At our table the women chatted warmly with two officer friends who kept their voices deep; my brother and I needed only to be polite and quiet. Fine. Later, we knew, we'd hear the officers being taken apart.

After lunch everybody jostled goodnaturedly down a hall hung with large framed photographs of military men and into a slope-floored room with rows of grey-velvet armchairs. The six of us sat about halfway up from the screen, I in the aisle seat, stick on lap, Jerry next to me. Around us men and women settled in with sighs and smiles, lit cigarettes: a good lunch, and now a film. Even after the lights went out they buzzed on a bit.

First News. A man's voice shouting, blasts of music, and grainy film showing parked airplanes, skyscrapers, tanks trailing dust, bowler-hatted men waving from a balcony, a tugboat in flames, soldiers marching, a limping runner, a pretty woman in a swimsuit, bouncing kangaroos, soccer players in the rain. The News always came first in cinemas (in Singapore before *Hotel Berlin*, in London before *Pinocchio* and *Road to Morocco*), and you had to sit through it.

Then the Feature Film. Or was it? No music, no title, no actors' names . . . grainy film of armed soldiers again . . . soundlessly they plodded along an empty road, no, not a road, a rail-

road track. *More* News? No, not News, something else . . . the
soldiers were approaching a high wire fence with, inside it, long
low buildings and, stretching into fog, all around, treeless
rolling fields. Then, suddenly, we were lurching in silence
through open barbed-wire gates, the picture wobbling on the
screen, towards a huddle of men in loose rags. Their faces came
right up to us, filling the screen, dark holes for mouths and eyes
set in stubbly wide-eared skulls. We looked from one to the next
to the next, eased through them, then almost stumbled over
several men lying queerly on the ground. We stopped and
looked at those men closely, slowly moving from one to the next,
from head to toes—none wore shoes. They lay still in watery
mud and had clothes missing, too, trousers, a shirt, and their
white skin showed black spots, sores maybe. One lay spread on
his back, mouth open, naked, and him we scanned almost inch
by inch—the bones jutting out of his white loose skin, his pri-
vates, the sticks that were his arms and legs. Then, as if needing
to take a little breath, we looked away and up and ahead, and
saw we were on a long narrow misty field with the low buildings
stretching on either side. As far as we could see, far back into
the haze, the field showed more clumps of men in rags, some
sitting, some standing, and more single ones lying down. Then
a man's voice said softly, oh, almost dreamily, that what we were
seeing was what the first Allied soldiers entering this place saw
and filmed. This was *such-and-such,* a Nazi concentration camp,
and the Nazis had murdered *this-many* men here. Millions of
men and women and children had been murdered in camps like
this. The exact number killed wasn't known yet, said the voice,
and might never be known. And that's all the voice said for a
while—and we wandered further into the field. Of the sitting
and standing men most were watching us, but a few craned

their necks like birds looking to the side or up at the sky, or they had turned their backs. They sat or stood very still, but now and then a man might make with an arm or a leg or his head a small jerky useless move. Not one came towards us. In a sitting group, a man sagged sideways, his head flopping into the mud, but the others took no notice. The voice murmured that for some of the living men we were looking at now, release had come too late: they would be dead soon. To our left up ahead was a doorway to one of the low buildings. Prisoner living quarters, said the voice. We neared it, entered, and for a few seconds the screen went black—then shadows showed, and in quickly growing hard brightness we saw tiers of rough wooden bunks, water glinting on the floor. Glancing left and right we slowly moved down the barrack, and skulls, hundreds of skulls looking alike whatever their age, watched us over the edges of the bunks, some working their mouths so we saw the broken teeth, some turning birdlike away, some clawing out at us. The faces looked vacant, or afraid or crazy or both. A man with a wispy beard hunkered on the path between the bunks, knees poking through ripped pants, feet swaddled in strips of muddy cloth. He was slowly shaking his head back and forth looking up at us. We leaned in very close and peered into the dark holes that were his eyes from which tears welled up and ran down his cheeks. The holes filled the screen—and I tasted vomit. The streaming holes were pulling at me, pulling me inside, pulling me into what lived there. *Oh no! Not me!* I shut my eyes tight, heaved forward, and didn't breathe. I was trembling. This was dangerous. The only sound in the little theatre was the projector's soft whirring. I breathed out but stayed still; sweat drops slid from my hair down my neck. I did not feel remote. I did not move, not until I finally *had* to look at Jerry. He sat as I did, perhaps had been for minutes already, and he'd stuck his fingers in his ears. I did the same. And so he and I stayed through the rest of the film stiffly saying No to going back where we had been.

Light reddened our eyelids and we sat up and put our hands down. Had anyone noticed? Men and women around us rose, blew noses, and, without even a whisper, began shuffling out. No one spoke in the taxi either; the women stared out the windows. At the hostel we said thank you for the lunch and thank you for the movie and they gave us small sorry smiles.

Jerry was so angry his lips quivered. Stupid! They were stupid to have let us see that film! How could they have? All the rest of that afternoon into early evening he fumed about "those stupid cows." But had the women known what would play? They'd said they didn't. Had anyone known in that still audience? The film *cut* Jerry, though, no question—for weeks afterwards he'd wake up in our bed soaked with sweat and shaking from nightmares. Our mother let us talk, didn't say much but, after the usual all-boiled dinner, wondered if maybe I'd like to go get a treat. She fished coins from her purse for chips, and I grabbed my stick and coat.

Chips were at Brooke Street's second crossroad, a five-minute trot away. In the feeble street-lighting the sidewalk glittered; it had been raining, of course, and puddles had formed. The going took longer because I had to gallop from puddle to puddle, whop them with my stick, and then jump them—but from a stand-still position, no run-up. To reach the other side safely spelled good luck, if not, well, even Jerry still liked stomping water. In the warm chip shop smelling of oil, adult customers crowded in front of the high white enamel counter. I had to push in and stand on tiptoe to reach the vinegar and salt; then I hurried out and ran home to keep the chips hot.

The treat was just for Jerry and me and we divided the chips exactly, counting, as we ate them one by one. Then we said good nights and undressed on our side of the curtain. I was already in pyjamas when I missed it. Was my stick on her bed I called to my mother. No. On the dresser? No, and not on the washstand either. When did I have it last, she asked. I'd smacked the puddles, then I was standing on my toes. . . . Oh *no*, I'd put it down on the counter to sprinkle vinegar and salt in the cone.

Both of you dress and go get it, our mother ordered from her bed. Minutes later we ran panting into the shop, empty just then, but the shiny-faced man behind the counter said yawning, No, he hadn't seen a stick. It had a dog's head, sir. Could somebody have taken it, sir? *His* customers? No.

And we were back in the damp outside. Maybe I'd dropped it running home, Jerry suggested. No, I was sure I'd left it on the counter. I was tasting vomit again. We should check anyway, Jerry said. So plodding back to the hostel, we scanned the sidewalk as we used to for money. But no. My mother promised that in the morning she'd stop by the shop herself. That's all, really, she could do, *liefje*. And if it didn't show up, well, I could pick out a new one, yes? No thank you, I said. I couldn't even imagine it. The two of them said soft things I didn't really hear, and then we went to bed.

In the dark next to Jerry I could see my hand laying the stick on top of the greasy counter. I felt someone else's eyes on it, and on me. I saw myself shaking vinegar and salt on the chips, then turning, and rushing out the door. The stick, alone, looked so forgotten that I felt one or two tears pressing out. The someone, a man, waited to see if anyone else noticed. Right then he should've handed it to the counter man—"A boy left this." Instead, eyes watchful, he covered the stick with his arm, drew it off the counter, fumbled it inside his coat, and then quickly left the shop, too. Outside, he probably started running, heart pounding, giggling, into moist darkness where rats lived. But after a while he slowed to an amble, swinging my stick and, as people said "Nice stick you have!" smiling thank you. So the bastard would walk the streets of London for I don't know how long until one day he stumbled and fell under the wheels of a fast-moving double-decker bus and squirting black-red blood was squashed to death flat as a sixpence.

Jerry and my mother let me be as they, and my father, too, had done just after the war, in Tjimahi, when I'd had weeping spells for dead Hubie. Except for the couple of tears in bed, I didn't cry for the stick; inside, though, just as with Hubie, I howled. The stick had been a part of me, had been, as on the fantasy Tarzan-swings, a friend on every imagined adventure; I'd seen myself carrying it as a man. Yet, as if the stick could help it, I blamed it, too: you could not trust things.

It was mid-February and a newspaper reported that bananas had arrived. We never saw one, but around that time the hostel did serve each of us an orange, and later an apple, the only fresh fruit we'd eat in poor England. Until we left London in early March, I, like the thief, walked the wintry streets. I looked for him every day. He was out there—on the sidewalk, in a store, an alley, at a bus stop, or maybe hiding the stick inside a long military overcoat. A soldier in uniform wouldn't have stolen it—only officers could carry one—but demobilized men wore the brownish green coats, too, for their warmth. The sidewalks teemed with ex-soldiers, scruffy many of them, some with an eye patch or a pinned-up sleeve, or on crutches, or with a terribly scarred face, and some drunk, or asleep in a doorway, or begging. Damaged heroes. People hurrying along London's sidewalks gradually seemed to take less notice—so *many* half-men were home from the war. Still, I gave them a once-over, too, to check for my stick. The thief was everywhere.

I looked for him when Jerry, to cheer me up, took me along to visit his good shipmate, Bill the joker. Bill lived somewhere on the edge of London on a treeless street in his parents' small house in the middle of a long "barrack" of attached, exact lookalikes. Inside the house it was chilly and damp; doilies and little rugs clung to the furniture and, mounted on the walls, china figurines and plates hung in rows. But Bill and his plump, cardiganed mum and dad seemed to live in the kitchen—steam-filled that afternoon from something white boiling in a big pot on the stove. We sat around the kitchen table drinking tea, Jerry and I waiting for jokes; clean jokes, of course, with the old people there. This restless rough young soldier had been famous on board for his crazy jokes and, after each telling, his own huge enjoyment of them, and he'd earned my lonely brother's friendship by looking at stars with him on Indian Ocean nights. He was telling us now that Mum had embroidered that tablecloth herself, and that, same as Dad, he worked in a vegetable market. It *was* early days there, at the market, but it wasn't messy, or smelly, and fair pay, and close by, and every other Saturday off. In the month he'd been home from the war, Bill had lost his thick red moustache—and maybe his wild old laughing self too. My brother and I drank our tea and left early.

Hunting the thief another time in late afternoon, I wandered into a quiet street, the roadway intact and cleared of rubble, but with most of the houses on either side gutted by bombs. A few had been sliced right down the middle, leaving the deserted halves looking like the open mouths of caves. It was raining, not an honest Java downpour, but the London way, thinly, unending. I was poking along when a tall American soldier caught up and looped past me. Americans wore the best-fitting uniforms, starched and pressed, and, with an easy sureness all their own, really looked like conquerers—not just of the enemy, but of everybody, of the world. Well-fed, cheerful, noisy, they chewed gum, whistled after women, wore hair cropped short as mine, and wrote things like *Hubba-hubba* on public walls. I didn't know any, but I liked them.

Up ahead, halfway along the street, the American suddenly stopped, lowered himself on a hunk of concrete that had been a stoop and lit a cigarette. Why sit down in the rain for a smoke? As I got closer he shifted for comfort, crossed his legs. Then he looked in my direction and smiled, showing fine American teeth.

"Hi!"

I'd heard many Americans say that.

Hi, sir.

He looked younger than my father, with white-blond hair, a wide, friendly mouth, but a London-pale face.

"Howrya?"

They said that, too.

Good, sir.

In England it was best to say sir or ma'am to strangers.

Where was I going?

Just walking, sir.

Faded blue eyes looked me up and down.

Was I English?

No, sir.

Where from then?

Java, sir.

So I was Dutch.

He may have been the first person in London who immediately connected Java with Dutch. Certainly no Red Cross woman or bride ever had; even the soldiers on the ship seldom did.

Yes, sir.

Good people, the Dutch. Smart. Good-looking.

He held out a pack of Camels, my father's brand.

Smoke?

No one had ever told me not to speak to strangers, not on the plantation, not in the camps, not on the ship. Strangers were people I didn't know—that's why they were interesting.

Yes, thank you, sir.

He may also have been the first person in London to offer me a cigarette. We knew mostly women and they just didn't.

I shouldn't call him "sir," he said. Americans didn't say "sir." He was Michael—Mike to his friends. I should say Mike.

Okay, Mike.

And my name?

Ernest.

Ernie—he stuck out his hand and I shook it. A big hand, warm and dry. He didn't look at me, though, shaking hands. Mostly his eyes roamed around as we talked. Maybe he was going to meet someone.

What was I doing in London?

Waiting to go to Canada.

Canada! Don't go to Canada, Ernie! he said. Canada was cold as hell. Bears and snow. Nope, I should go to the States. Best place on earth, the States. Everybody had a house, a dog, a car, a swimming pool. He was from California—beaches, you know, sun, beautiful girls.

Hollywood? I said, and in the moist air blew a little smoke ring.

I was quite a smoker, Mike said. I smoked like a man. Yep, Hollywood, you bet. Film stars. Betty Grable. Rita Hayworth. Did I like beautiful women? He was sure I did.

Yes, I said.

It was nice to be talking to a man again and smoking, even if it was cold standing still.

Well, he'd seen that right away, that I liked girls. Yep, my big brown eyes said so. Americans called women "dames," did I know that? American dames were the best in the world, you know. Gorgeous, very friendly. If I came to visit him in California, he'd introduce me to lots of them. That was a promise, okay?

Okay!

He himself knew many women, the ones in California, and here in London, too. He knew so many, you know, that he sometimes got tired of them. Honest. He wished, Mike said, suddenly sounding a little sad, that he was home. He missed America. He missed, you know, his friends, his buddies. In London he didn't have any buddies. Women were great, but buddies, well, buddies were the best.

In the wet rubble he went on a little about buddies, how he missed them, how one buddy was worth ten dames, and I thought I saw smouldering in his eyes the "deep look" some soldiers had, my mother had told me, from having seen much pain and death. But then he said that doctors had forbidden him to fight and he worked in a military office in London—so that couldn't be.

Did I have buddies? he asked, looking down the empty street one way, and then the other. Light was thinning.

Just my brother.

How old was he?

Fifteen.

Nice guy?

Yep.

Where was he now?

Probably reading.

I enjoyed the questions. People didn't often ask me questions.

Why was I going to Canada?

My mom was Canadian.

Was she with us?

Yep.

Should we have one more smoke? A dry one? Mike asked, and he stood up.

Sure.

He turned and strode off into the blasted debris behind us towards the nearest half-house, and I stumbled after him. Inside, in near darkness, he eased aside dangling beam stumps and pipes and, after slapping it clean with his handkerchief, sat down on the third step of a staircase with the bottom steps missing. I heaved up next to him, my feet just off the ground; ahead I could still make out a patch of street. The ruin smelled of burnt wood, cloth, rubber; water dripped; the hum of the city was entirely shut out. Mike's lighter flicked and he lit both our cigarettes.

Wasn't this like a secret cave? he said, his voice sounding suddenly deeper.

He didn't speak for a few moments. I could hear him smoking, hear his clothes rustle. It was as chilly inside as out on the street.

He was going to be honest, Mike said. He missed the States, all right, but, you know, Ernie, he didn't get along there very well. Sure, he'd told me he had a lot of buddies in California, but he didn't, not really.

I said nothing. Mike and buddies!

He had no buddies over there, at home, and none over here. And yet, you know, he was a nice guy. He *was* a nice guy, wasn't he?

Yep, I said.

I liked saying "yep" and "nope." Punchy.

The reason he had no buddies was complicated, Mike went on, his cigarette between his lips. The reason was, well, did I know the reason? Could I guess?

Nope.

No idea?

Nope.

Not at all?

Nope.

I looked ahead and, *oh, oh*—I couldn't see the street any more. My mother wouldn't worry about a few minutes, though. Mike coughed, or that's what it sounded like.

He wanted to ask me a question, a serious question, he said, the cigarette still in his mouth. Did I like him?

Sure.

And then I felt his big warm dry hand curving over my knee and my thigh.

That's good, he said quietly.

His hand moved not at all. We sat like that for maybe a minute, maybe longer. I didn't like or dislike the hand there, but it felt a little strange.

That's really good, he said.

In the blackness only the tips of our cigarettes showed. I had to get back to the hostel for dinner. I slipped out from under his hand and jumped off the step.

I was going home, I said.

Okay.

I couldn't see him and I couldn't hear him move; maybe I heard him sigh.

"Seeya," Mike said.

Americans said that, too.

I left him sitting alone in the dark in the half-house, his secret cave, and ran home.

My mother said nothing about my being late. She had news, she announced, so we gulped down our boiled evening meal with the brides. Up in the attic on her bed, shoes off, she reported that, number one, our father had written that right now he couldn't send money because of the fighting, the "revolution," though he was sure he'd be able to soon. That was troubling because the Red Cross wouldn't hand out pounds forever. But, two, her friend the colonel's advice had worked just right. He'd told her to quit hounding the British government for help; it was useless. Instead, she should ask her father to sponsor a year's visit and lend her the fare; once in Canada, she could pay him back when money came free in Indonesia. Well, after a lot of cables and letters, Grampa had said yes and so, finally, had the Canadian government. The next hurdle was "Priority"—permission to ship out ahead of thousands of others waiting as anxiously as we were, including Canadian soldiers and brides from all over. Her Canadian birth and the prison-camp years had helped a lot. Boys, we're going, she said smiling, *we are!* She grabbed our faces and kissed our foreheads. We're *going!* Jerry and I thumped each other and let out Tarzan yells, and there was no shushing.

Tea, we needed tea. In stocking feet she ran down four flights and scrounged mugs of tea. Back on her bed, she said, I'll tell you about Canada, and she did as she'd never done before. We'd always heard just snippets about what she missed and then the stuff she'd told the brides. But now she talked like a giddy girl. She talked as if she had been there yesterday, as if she hadn't been gone longer than Jerry's whole life. She talked, yes exactly, like soldiers on hot decks—home, going bloody home!

Oh we'd love Canada! We'd see it all! London rain softly tapped the roof as she spun on and on about whatever tripped into her mind. About Toronto in white, Toronto in green, and Toronto in flames in autumn. About sweet-tempered horses that pulled milk wagons along streets at dawn knowing precisely at which houses to stop as drivers trotted up and down lawns delivering fresh milk in bottles. About the boardwalk by flat grey cold Lake Ontario. About her mother's double-crusted rice pudding. About streetcars that ding-dinged so *politely.* About popcorn, popsicles, and pop. About cutting through Ames Bush just in bathing suits and raincoats to go swimming at the Beach. About 11 Osborne Avenue, her home, where we'd live now, have our own room. About Christmas windows downtown. About Queen Victoria Day fireworks. About squirrels in Kew Gardens. About all the chewing gum under the seats of the Ideal Theatre on Main. About roasting chestnuts. About "those characters," her family—and down the long list she went saying how good and smart and funny and *interesting* they were, how

happy they'd be to see us, Grampa, Gramma, Aunty Ada, Uncle
Alfred. . . . About her old schools—our schools now—Kimberley
Public School and Malvern Collegiate. We'd play baseball and
hockey and tennis. We'd make friends, Canadian friends, lots
and lots of Canadian friends. . . . I wondered sleepily if Mike was
still sitting on the broken stairs in the dark. Or was he roaming
the streets, smokes ready, looking for a buddy? Lonely, lonely . . .
lots and lots of Canadian friends . . .

The brides might have resented our Priority, so we said goodbye
to only a few of them and on March 7 tiptoed out of the hostel
at dawn—on the go again. We'd had to wait too long in grey
London, its beautiful oldness unminded: to us it was just a wet
shut-in place to get out of. The taxi to the station and the train
back to Liverpool couldn't go fast enough. Left fluttering
behind were "Alien," boiled food, brides, rain, fog, Red Cross
women, Madame Tussaud, Mike, the skulls, and even the stick,
the thief, and military overcoats.

Along with hundreds of other civilians, most in ill-fitting
clothes, lugging string-tied sacks and carton boxes, we boarded
the SS *Cavina* in late afternoon. People around us spoke softly
in strange languages, mostly French and Polish, we learned
later. The British liner's steel outside was flecked with rust.
Inside, we queued up on worn carpeting in a lounge where
unsmiling stewards handed out berth and dining-table numbers. One barked that men and women must sleep in separate
quarters, no mixing, was that clear? Did aliens annoy all
Englishmen?

"I married," said a passenger, but was quickly cut off: that
was the rule. A nonsense rule, it turned out—there were many
two-bunk cabins and not many married couples.

Ernest with swagger stick, 1946

*Anna Hillen in her Oxford Street
fedora, London, 1946*

*Jerry had learned to read English in
the month at sea, 1946*

Canada bound on the Cavina, March 1946

The Watson home on Osborne Avenue, Toronto, 1946

Toronto Daily Star photo, March 21, 1946, that accompanied interview with Anna Hillen

IT'S A DELAYED Christmas for Mrs. John Hillen, Osborne Ave., and her sons, Gerald and Ernest. They've just arrived home after almost four years in Jap internment camp in Batavia where they ate cats, dogs, rats and snails for their Christmas dinners

Harry and Mabel Watson

Spring 1946, in the Watson backyard: Ernest, Gramma, Grandpa, Jerry

Ernest, age twelve

Glen Holway, 1947

*Niagara Falls outing,
1946: Anna Hillen,
Ernest, Ralph Holway,
Ada, Shirley Ann, Glen
(Jerry took the picture)*

*Moving to the Kingston
Road cabin, 1946*

*The brothers loaded with
borrowed sports equipment,
in front of the cabin, 1947*

Birthday gift picture sent to John Hillen in Indonesia, 1947

*John Hillen at work,
Batavia (Jakarta),
Indonesia, 1947*

Ernest at summer's end, 1947

Our mother shared one of the two-bunkers with the only English woman on board, and Jerry and I a musty four-bunker with two Poles, one married, and the other, a cheerful, short, bald bachelor. They spoke no English, came in only after the bar closed singing softly, staggered around undressing, and snored. The single man, using his hands and watch and a smile, asked us the second day if, from two to three that afternoon, he might have the cabin to himself. We said sure. The next day, from eleven to noon, yes? Then two to three again, then four to five, and so on, every day across the North Atlantic. The married Pole never asked for privacy.

But who cared? Rough weather hit the moment we left port and raged the entire ten days; if seasickness gets bad enough, all you want is to be alone in the dark. Most passengers looked glum, from the crazy pitching, but really, even on boarding they'd seemed downhearted. The mood never lifted. People stuck mostly to their cabins; the lounges, bar, and dining room never filled; there was no music, no singing, no dancing. They had probably come through bad times, my mother said, the war, camps, death—look at their eyes—and they were poor. But weren't they going to Canada? Wouldn't everything be fine in Canada? Maybe, but what were they leaving behind? Country, family, friends, language, home, possessions. Well, I thought, Jesus, *we* didn't mope.

Or act weird either. Besides my brother and me, there was only one other big kid on board, a Polish boy my age who once or twice gave me a shy smile. I might've liked to play with him— Jerry had gone to live in the library—but he never left his mother's side. She was a heavy woman always dressed in a bulky red sweater and man's trousers, who liked to plop down in a lounge and quietly play cards and sip drinks with other women.

They drank sweet vermouth; the boy, too, as he stood or sat leaning against his mother, not speaking, half-asleep. He had a thin face, red-veined brown eyes, and wore a brown cloth cap with ear flaps, even inside.

One afternoon I saw his mother playing with just the other women there—my chance to find the kid alone. But just then he rushed into the lounge, looked wildly around, spotted his mother, ran over, squirmed in beside her, and, just like that, took hold of one of her big breasts. He fondled the breast, squeezing it, stroking it, until she absently brushed his hand away; the other women also stayed deep in the game. I wouldn't, of course, even talk to him after that—grabbing his mom's tit!—though I queasily watched him do it again several times. How bloody *could* he? Did all Poles do that? No, my mother said, of course not. The poor boy had probably once had a horrible fright or a shock or something—God knows what happens in war. I remembered little round wounds and scars on pale arms. But not to worry, she said, he'd eventually get over it. Freaky just the same, though.

Because of seasickness I tried to stay on deck—*seeing* the wild water helped—but it was often too cold. Other passengers did, too, but few lasted long, except for two who, no matter how the wind howled, always ignored it. Arms tight around each other, laughing, they scrambled from handhold to handhold down sloshing decks and then, suddenly, in the warren of derricks, air ducts, and lifeboats, they'd be gone. A young man and woman, French and tanned and inseparable, although I happened to see them come aboard singly. Every day they murmured for hours in a corner of the bar, faces close, never looking away. So quiet and caught up they were—yet everyone kept an eye on them, not just me. "Lovey-doveys" my mother called them. Mid-morning and sometimes mid-afternoon as well, they'd do the disappearing trick, and not show up until lunch or dinner. They would rise from their table, give a little kiss, and hurry swaying to their separate cabins. Minutes later, in overcoats, they'd meet again at a certain deck-door, wrestle it open, and lunge out into the cold. I'd followed them a few times, for something to do, but had always been given the slip. One stormy day I timed it and hid in a windless nook midship behind the bridge near where I'd lost them before. And sure, there they came swinging along, bodies pressed close, hair flying, and by the bow of a lifeboat they dove out of sight. I crept closer and peeked from behind the next boat. What they'd done, so clever and strictly against the rules, was untie a corner of their boat's canvas hood. I watched as he gently hoisted her inside and then climbed in after. His hand came back out and tugged the overhead canvas neatly in place. It had to be cozy inside. Did they have a blanket in there? Did time go fast for them? With every plunge into the cold rough sea, the tired ship was carrying them closer to Canada.

FOUR / A Family Like in a Book

THE LAND WASN'T CHOCOLATE BROWN at all, but white—dazzling blinding white in the Canadian morning sun as the *Cavina* steamed honking into Halifax harbour. That was snow on the ground and on the trees, on all the unharmed buildings and houses and churches, on the docks and cranes and a hundred moored ships. Real goddamn *snow*! The air cracked with cold, but the snow looked warm; inside the snow it had to be warm. Standing in the bow, our mother clutched our hands and softly, sing-songily repeated, "Canada, boys! You're looking at *Canada*!" The ocean's temper was behind us, the wind still, the water smooth. Passengers quietly crowded the decks, many coatless—I hadn't noticed that when they trudged on board in Liverpool; no wonder so few ever came up top. The men wore fedoras or drab cloth caps like the Polish boy's, the women kerchiefs. They looked at what we were looking at, but their eyes didn't spark. That's Canada, people! I thought. *Cheer up*! During breakfast the loudspeaker had said that, with some exceptions, everyone must report to Pier 21. We three were among the exceptions—not DPs any more, nor Immigrants; we were Visitors. Pier 21ers, we heard later, would be sorted, questioned, and some, for "government reasons," promptly shipped back. Canada was careful, and maybe many of those glum passengers knew that.

Inside a cloud of screaming Canadian seabirds, tugboats pulled the ship to the docks and there quick men tied her down. I eyed the white city with concentration and, with my mind's eye, the white land beyond. It was crazy, but in those minutes I tried as hard as I could to "float" high up so that, even though I knew its enormity from a map, I could "take in" the *whole* country— mountains, rivers, prairies, lakes, forests, cities, farms, igloos, trains, cars, dogsleds, bears, wolves, moose, foxes, people, the lot. I wanted to *own* Canada a little before stepping ashore. It didn't work, though *likenesses* of it all flickered furiously.

The engines shut off and with a sigh the ship shuddered into silence. Passengers haltingly started down the gangplank, most of them, including our Polish cabin mates, the boy and his mother, and the French couple, tramping off for Pier 21, wher- ever that was. Not us. We put our Visitors' feet on Canada, a taxi pulled up, and we coolly got in and drove away—why not, we had money. Three days earlier, though, we didn't: no money for treats on board, for steward tips, for a taxi to the railway station, or for train fare to Toronto. Grampa Watson had wired the ship's passage fee all right, but just precisely that, forgetting— how could he?—the overland trip still to come; and also, though there'd been lots of time, his money was received in last-minute panic in Liverpool just before sailing. Out at sea our mother counted the pennies left from her Red Cross savings. She worried for days and finally nervously asked to borrow money from the Captain at whose table she'd already eaten twice, and he immediately said yes. Jerry and I only learned of all this months later—why spoil *our* trip?

We were early at the station, so there was time for a quick first walk in Canada. The sunlit street was edged with grey ice and piles of snow no one played on; the snow tasted gritty, crunched underfoot, and made fine hard balls; snowballs were best moulded with bare hands and they exploded on the target. From roofs and walls, coloured signs cheered us on to Drink! Chew! Smoke! Eat! Clean! Brush! Save! Drive! Enjoy! Own! Buy! In one shop window teetered *pyramids* of apples, oranges, grapefruit, and bananas; another glistened with *stacks* of bloody meat and slick plucked chickens; a third was *crammed* with gleaming red-and-white bicycles, boxing gloves, and sports stuff our mother had to explain—baseball bats and gloves, skis and poles, hockey sticks, egg-shaped footballs. But it was at a tobacconist, after hot begging, that money was spent—twenty cents on two Tarzan *comic books*! Cars in daring colours crowded the road, most much bigger than in London but with only the driver inside; people looked bulkier in their overcoats, and women's faces were often hidden inside fur-trimmed hoods; everyone wore boots. As in London, people hurried along, eyes flat ahead; and so amazing—we saw no ruins, rubble, shabby military overcoats, or half-men.

The *Nova Scotian* pulled out an hour later and, seldom stopping, hurtled through the countryside all that afternoon and night and the next day and night. Now and then it sounded a lovely lonely wail. In our roomette, we spoke little, stared out at the white land flying by—telephone poles, frozen forests and rivers and fields, sleeping villages and farms—read, played cards, dozed, slept. What were all those dots over there in the snow? Jerry asked once. The tops of fenceposts, our mother said. The long hours clattered by and each of us had to be thinking of what was coming: she had an idea; we didn't really. Before any big change our mother had always promised it was an adventure; she'd said so even the night before going into camp. But she didn't say it on the train. What was coming, what we were careening towards, was 7:15 a.m., Union Station, Toronto, journey's end, her waiting family, promised days of "normal living."

Hugs, no kisses, she told us, applying lipstick in the roomette's dancing mirror. She blotted off most of the red on toilet paper, then fussily daubed on more. It was just seven but we'd already put our coats on—"Do it, dammit! I've got butterflies!" Up since God knows when herself, she'd woken us at 5:30 and ordered a washing in the tiny sloshing sink—crotch, armpits, *feet*; my brother and I weren't friendly in that small shaking space. She'd also insisted on fresh underwear, shirts, socks, and finally that we spit on our shoes and, with yesterday's socks, rub them shiny.

Working the lipstick, she prattled on that we were, of course, used to the Dutch kissing hello, but her family, well, just as they didn't cry, they didn't kiss. They never had. They might hug. To tell the truth, she couldn't really remember one of them ever kissing. So we shouldn't expect to get or to give kisses when we met them, only hugs, maybe. On second thought, she said, finally letting her lips be, it might be best if Jerry and I just shook hands, nothing more, and then, if anyone did decide to hug, to let them, but not to be the one to start. Her family were not cold people, we should understand, they just weren't dramatic people, they weren't kissers or, she supposed, really huggers either.

As it happened, that was pretty well true, at least where Jerry and I were concerned. With our mother it was hard to tell because she didn't follow her own advice. Not much of a kisser or hugger herself, she really let go in Toronto. We were coming down an escalator in that huge, high-ceilinged, hard-lit building, when suddenly she spotted them waiting gravely at the bottom—Grampa, Gramma, sister Ada, brother Alfred. Dropping her luggage she dashed ahead calling "Papa!" like a child and flung her arms around a slightly startled Grampa and kissed him smack on both cheeks, and then "Mama!", smack, smack, and on to "Ada!" and to "Alfred!" embracing them with grip, kissing, crying a little. Jerry and I stood and watched. She hadn't cried in years. It was all happening so fast—were they hugging her back, kissing her back, crying? I think they didn't have much choice, except for crying: no crying. Actually, they then started laughing—her, too, us, too—because all four had these deep-red smears on their cheeks. As our mother rubbed at their faces with her handkerchief, they shook hands with Jerry and me, and yes, Gramma and Aunty Ada did give us a little hug. What my new Canadian grandfather said shaking my hand unsmiling was, "So young fellow, what's your excuse?" Grampa would ask me that from then on almost every time he saw me, and I didn't, not in Union Station or ever later, have an answer.

They walked us out into Toronto sunshine and there, facing us across thick traffic, towered a real skyscraper. "The Royal York Hotel!" announced Uncle Alfred, and stopped to gaze up. He was a lanky, narrow-shouldered man, with our mother's freckles and red hair, who wore a bowler hat. We'd been told that for breakfast he would often just swallow a raw egg stirred in a glass. "That's the largest, tallest structure in the British Empire!" Uncle Alfred said. Well, Jerry and I had seen Buckingham Palace and Gibraltar—where was the snow? Toronto looked as whole as Halifax, but it had no snow!

We crossed the street—seven of us, all family!—for breakfast in a crowded restaurant smelling of fried bacon; the Honeydew was her favourite, Gramma said. Grampa, bald and a bit chubby, was the boss. He sat us down so we three, with our mother in the centre, faced the four of them, so nicely dressed, rings and earrings and dark suits with vests. Aunty Ada and our mother looked a lot like Gramma except that, while she had extremely blonde hair, Aunty Ada's was brown. Gramma had hazel eyes and the sisters soft brown ones; Grampa's were brown, almost black; Uncle Alfred's also hazel. Aunty Ada did look at Jerry and me once or twice, but really the family's eyes were fixed on their glowing-happy daughter and sister in her Oxford Street hat; their eyes ate her up a little.

Where were Ralph and Lois (Ada's husband and Alfred's wife) and their kids? our mother immediately wanted to know. She didn't, she joked, come home after sixteen years every day!

They smiled at that. Aunty Ada shyly, Gramma showing *perfect* teeth, Grampa and Uncle Alfred thinly; Uncle Alfred's smile revealed teeth, too, long ones, but Grampa's not, ever; I'd only see his teeth once.

Oh Ralph had badly wanted to come, said Aunty Ada, he really did, and Lois, too—but Papa wouldn't let them. Papa had first said it should be just him and Mama at the station. She and Alfred had argued *that,* and won, but Papa had still said no to Ralph and Lois. Papa had been a "pessimist" about how she, Anna, might look and feel, that she might be a wreck.

But hadn't anybody *read* her letters? our mother protested. She'd written dozens saying how okay we were. She plucked a ready slip of paper from her purse. Her *first* letter, she said, was dated August 28, 1945, and she'd written: "Here we are again! We are still among the living—the healthy and lucky living!" She looked at Grampa.

As if he hadn't heard her, or Aunty Ada, Grampa said, but he said it smiling, Well, she, Anna, might have stepped off the train in rags and damn well looked like "the Wreck of the Hesperus."

We'd often been told that Grampa had "a fine little sense of humour, but you had to get used to it."

Harry! Gramma said, chiding him but not really. And then Gramma said that she, Anna, looked just "fine and dandy." So healthy, so well-dressed, she couldn't get over it. It was for-goodness-sake amazing! She had honestly not expected that, and it was for her, for them all, such a relief!

My new Canadian grandmother leaned back then and lit a DuMaurier.

"You're a sight for sore eyes, Anna," said Grampa, and lit a cigar.

"Amen," said Uncle Alfred.

Aunty Ada slid a little package across, a present. Excited, our mother unwrapped it—a pair of earrings. She leaned over the table and kissed her sister saying, thank you, thank you.

It was nothing, said Aunty Ada.

A waitress in a yellow dress served coffee and tea and took our food orders.

No one had anything to say for a few moments. Grampa and Gramma smoked.

How bad was it? Uncle Alfred finally asked, and that may have been the only question that morning; none, anyhow, about the Batavia–Toronto trip, our father, or the plantation; no questions, certainly, of Jerry and me.

Our mother told them about the camps, in her way. Sure, we'd been hungry, and there was no medicine, and the Japanese could be mean, but she didn't go into details, told few pain-and-death stories. She talked instead about how camp life brought people closer, often making them stronger, more generous; you used your common sense, you tried to laugh, you looked out for each other. I must say the family listened— Uncle Alfred staring over her head, smiling a little; Grampa's dark eyes on her unblinking; Aunty Ada and Gramma chirping Canadian expressions of wonder such as "gee!" "gosh!" "for Pete's sake!" "for crying out loud!" "I'll be darned!" and "holy cow!"

She, Anna, might be asked to make speeches, Grampa said suddenly.

Yes, Uncle Alfred agreed with his father.

(She was, too, after a radio station called CFRB interviewed her two days later and the *Toronto Daily Star* wrote a story because she was the first civilian home from a "Jap camp"— TURKEY TASTES GOOD AFTER CATS, RATS AND DOGS.)

Grampa and Uncle Alfred "had the brains in the family," our mother had often told us. They never said much, so we should listen when they did. They were good men, smart men. Gramma and Aunty Ada, of course, were kind women, loving women. They might be "characters," she'd said again and again, but her family was good and kind. It was a pleasure watching our new Canadian relatives eating pancakes drenched in "real Canadian" maple syrup. We had all ordered pancakes.

Then Aunty Ada and Uncle Alfred left to find his car: he had to go to his office; Grampa had taken the day off. I asked Gramma and she said, sure, everybody had their own car. Grampa's big pale-green one was parked around the corner, on Bay Street, but it was Gramma, a cigarette in her mouth, who got behind the wheel and drove us, with Grampa beside her, to Osborne Avenue.

She'd hardly stopped in front of the house—two storeys of red brick and green shutters, a veranda with white pillars, a white picket fence, a long brown lawn, several good Tarzan trees—when Jerry and I jumped out. For this moment we'd bought two firecrackers in London. We lit them as a few neighbours watched from porches. Fine bangs, laughter, applause, and shouts of "Welcome home!" Our mother asked in a small voice, "No flag, Papa?" but then marched ahead and opened Grampa's front door with a key she'd carried for sixteen years. Inside . . . a small dark linoleum-floored hall, a stairway . . . the bannister she'd slid down on as a girl! I rushed to try it, but behind me Gramma called, "Boots off, young man!" Boots? We didn't have boots. Then I heard Jerry say "Oh!" and turned and saw through an open door a huge Christmas tree sagging under red and silver decorations. I must have said "Oh!" too—glowing and sparkling, it was glorious. This was late March, so the tree had been waiting for us for three months. Tearing again, our mother said that's where she'd always imagined the Watson tree, right in that same old corner. The tree stood in a bucket of water and around the bucket in a bedding of dead needles lay some packages and a red-bowed sled. For us? Jerry asked softly. Yes, Gramma said, they've just been waiting for you boys.

In that warm airless room of browns and greys with the curtains drawn, Grampa dropped into one of two overstuffed armchairs and relit his cigar; Gramma sank into the other one. Each chair had a standing lamp beside it, piles of newspapers, magazines, and books, an ashtray balanced on the right arm, and, next to Grampa's, a tall upright radio. The chairs faced a small plain sofa across the room above which hung the one picture, a print of the faces of three curly-haired smiling child-angels. He now wanted a goddamn sleep, Grampa said, but, yes, the boys could first open their presents. We sat on the floor and tore off wrapping paper which our mother gathered and folded "for next Christmas"—a nice thought! Besides the sled, a base-ball bat and a softball, and, for each of us, a flannel sportshirt, a pair of thick socks, a pair of woollen gloves, and a scarf. The sleigh was the best, but no damn snow! We thanked with just plain thank-yous, no hugs or kisses. Now everybody get the hell out, said Grampa, and Gramma said, Harry!

Our mother carried her luggage upstairs on tiptoe, so we did, too. She said that in this house we had better learn to always walk softly, not to run, even barefoot, or wrestle, or shout. Noise upset Grampa and Gramma—they were in their mid-sixties—and it *was* their house. When she was a girl, Grampa used to yell from the hallway at bedtime, "I want silence up there, and mighty little of that!" My brother and I would try to keep it down, we really would try.

Jerry and I unpacked in the two front bedrooms—each as big as the London attic room!—and our mother in the one behind us; at the rear of the house was Grampa's and Gramma's bedroom. It turned out that they rose before us, and retired later, so we never really saw them upstairs—except a few times, a glimpse, on Saturday mornings when they slept late and one or the other would shuffle downstairs in robe and slippers and return to their room with two small glasses of whisky.

We wouldn't see much of them downstairs either. On day two the Christmas tree was dismantled and Jerry and I were seldom invited into the parlour again, and our mother not often. Grampa and Gramma liked to be alone there. They read a lot, smoked, and had short sleeps. In the evening of that second day Grampa showed something of his famous "cool customer" side. While Gramma was in the kitchen making coffee, Grampa dozed off and the butt of his cigar toppled from the ashtray onto the chair's arm. He woke up, looked at the smoke rising, but didn't move a muscle. "Mabel!" he roared, "get me a cup of water!" We heard him upstairs and came running down. Gramma rushed in with the cup. Grampa still sat slumped in place. He took the water, doused the smouldering hole, placed the ashtray over it, and handed the cup back to Gramma. Snapping open his paper, he growled, "Show's over!"

They read the *Globe and Mail*, the *Toronto Daily Star*, *Saturday Night*, the *Saturday Evening Post*, *Time*, and library books. Grampa never bought books because "they clutter up the place." CBL News was switched on at six or at ten o'clock, depending on when Grampa came home from the office. Jerry and I were told, also on day two, never to touch his radio. On the odd night they went out, though, our mother turned it on for us anyway and so, gradually, we entered the marvellous worlds of *The Shadow*, *Perry Mason*, *People Are Funny*, *Duffy's Tavern*, *Gangbusters*, *Dick Tracy*, *Terry and the Pirates*, *Abbott and Costello*, and *Boston Blackie*. Worlds that lingered long after because, as if you were blind, *seeing* them was done in your head.

The dining room became off limits as well. We ate supper there with the five of us until, after about two weeks, it was decided we three should eat first, in the kitchen, and Grampa and Gramma later, in the dining room—and we shared no more meals. This, it was said, was because Grampa needed peace and quiet after work, Jerry needed more time to study, and other reasons. But that wasn't why. Gramma, we learned much later, had told Grampa a little sadly that during meals he mostly conversed with Anna, hardly with her, and that she didn't like it. Grampa ordered separate suppers. In the big quiet house, that left just the beige and white kitchen where Gramma spent a lot of time and Grampa almost none.

That evening though, the evening of the first day, Gramma served a surprise Christmas dinner—turkey, cranberry sauce, mince pie. This had our mother in tears again, for the third time, and she made jabbery little thank-you remarks with almost every bite: oh those linen napkins! oh those sweet potatoes! sparkling glasses! red candles! green beans! salt and pepper shakers from when she was a girl! Aunt Helen's tablecloth! the gravy! the succotash! Grampa hurried her on and, sure, just as we finished, the doorbell rang. Surprise! Uncle Alfred's and Aunty Ada's families had come to visit. Our mother's eyes filled again—but that was the end of it. I, at least, saw no more tears for years.

Dining-room chairs were lugged into the parlour, and our complete Canadian family sat down on either side of Grampa and Gramma—ten altogether—opposite us three on the couch. A family like in a book. In moments tobacco smoke swirled like mist. The new faces were Uncle Alfred's Lois, Sandra, six, and Michael, three, and Aunty Ada's Ralph Holway, Shirley Ann, seventeen, and Glen, fourteen. Jerry and I were a bit overwhelmed—so much family! And I also felt a little shrunken, a little *less*, in their midst because they seemed, even the little kids, so entirely *comfortable*. This feeling would persist with Aunty Ada's family even after we got to know them better and shared good times. I don't know why. Uncle Alfred's family we rarely met again; never saw the inside of his house: he wasn't a "mixer," our mother explained.

Camp stories were what they wanted to hear, and she obliged, but of course they weren't as fresh as they had been in the Honeydew. The listening was as intent and polite as that morning with again no questions but lots of gees and goshes and now also a few Holy Christs from Uncle Ralph. No conversation, though: our mother did the talking. Bright, very attentive eyes, those of the family's adults, but no, nothing smouldered in them. Uncle Ralph, whose eyes did sparkle, gave quiet Jerry and me a cheery thumbs-up once or twice; he had a small crisp moustache like Mr. Otten the boar killer's. So wordless were Aunt Lois and her little kids, and Shirley Ann, a very pretty "older" girl who already wore lipstick and had a bad cold, you almost forgot they were there. Not so cousin Glen, although he said nothing either. Big as a man, he shifted restlessly on his straight chair, eyes roving, energy wafting off him. I don't think he was bored; it was having to sit still. We looked alike: large brown eyes, brushcuts, chunky bodies, mine much smaller of course. I watched how, when his father uttered a Holy Christ, Glen *shot* him a look. When Uncle Ralph reacted once with, "Incredible, Anna—and I mean that sincerely!" his son snorted. Shaking hands earlier, Uncle Ralph had greeted me: "Glad to meet you, Ernie—and I mean that sincerely!" I thought it a friendly thing to say.

Suddenly Glen rose mumbling he needed a drink of water, and edged out of the parlour. In the dining room he turned and jerked his head just at me to follow. I got up and said I wanted water, too. In the kitchen, though, Glen wasn't at the sink, he was gently lifting the latch of the side door.

"A man's gotta have his smoke, eh?" he whispered, grinning, but alert: it was a little test.

Yep, I said.

And then we were out in the dark trotting on frozen grass to the rear of the yard. There was the shed, now caved-in, where once my mother secretly wrote young-girl stories. Glen quickly, expertly rolled a cigarette. Manang, our gardener on the plantation, used to do that. Like a cowboy, Glen fired a wooden match with his thumb.

Goddamn! he needed that, he said dragging deeply. I didn't smoke yet, did I?

Yep, I said, looking up at this wide-shouldered, brand-new cousin.

But I was only eleven.

Twelve in two weeks, I said.

Well, holy shit, said Glen, and got out his tobacco and papers again. It was about eight o'clock and already very still. Twelve wasn't a bad age to start, Glen allowed. Then he handed me the thin, twisted cigarette and snapped a match for it. The last time I'd smoked was with Mike the American in London.

Okay, cousin?

Yep.

Very okay. The best present that day was not the sleigh, it was Glen's roll-your-own. Glen singling me out was by far the warmest bloody welcome-to-Canada! That feeling I'd had with the family in the parlour, the feeling of being less? With Glen alone—poof! gone!

To make a friend, I remembered, was absolutely dangerous: friends never lasted. With Glen the fear melted—maybe *because* he seemed so comfortable. I would for a time try to be Glen. He could do no wrong and everything about him seemed worthy and so worth copying. I would try to walk, talk, laugh, dress, shoot looks, brush teeth, polish shoes, do push-ups, and think as he did. His likes, dislikes, and purposes I made mine. We wouldn't see each other that often, really, but when we did— always at his home on Pine Glen Road, usually on Sundays—I, too, loathed his mother's spinach-cheese soufflé, loved toasted brown-sugar sandwiches, and blithely inhaled the powerful rank smell of his room. After supper we'd take Patchy, a happily clumsy spaniel, for a walk; Glen usually preferred to be out of his father's house. Talking and smoking, we'd wander down to Queen Street. (Jerry seldom joined us: he'd find a quiet place in the Holway home and read.) On the way, we passed a small park with benches and sometimes we sat down like old men. The questions came from me, the answers from Glen—private lessons in what came down to this: the way for a man. Glen knew. He'd been working on it for a long time. He was a kindly, patient instructor even though, early on, I must have seemed very dumb. As I slowly came to understand it, the task ahead was to find and then let ripen just precisely the right mix of "staying in shape," "getting girls," "independence," and "dressing in style"; I wasn't to worry yet about "making money." Glen shut up if we met any of his friends in the little "milkshake store" at Queen and Wineva. Meet my Dutch cousin, he'd say, and the older boys might nod, but I should then go and look at comic books. Fine: the friends were much like Glen, and I learned from them, too.

Now, in Grampa's backyard, Glen punched his hands deep in his pockets. No Canadian clothes yet, eh? he asked. Lesson number one had begun.

I looked down at myself.

I had to get some, Glen said, yeah, really, I had to get some Canadian clothes. Goddamn important, clothes; pants maybe the most. I needed new pants. Maybe I could get my mother to buy some.

My tweed plus-fours *were* big.

What he was wearing now, Glen said, pointing to his trousers, was the style. Everybody wore them. You *had* to. *He* had to, anyway. After school he worked in a grocery store, delivering, and he'd bought his first pair himself. Now he had three. Draped gabardine with, see, dropped belt loops and *outseams*. The style had been going a year, a year and a half now.

A *year and a half*! God, I wanted a pair of draped gabardine pants! I'd damn well *get* draped gabardine pants!

A belt, Glen said, yeah, I'd need a belt.

His was slim black leather with a small silver buckle. The buckle didn't sit above the fly as usual, but a loop away to the left.

Buckle always on the left, Glen said.

This was perfect. I was learning what to do.

Diamond socks and Loafers, Glen said, *polished* Loafers. Did I have running shoes?

Nope.

Well, I'd need running shoes for sports, and moccasins for casual.

Indian moccasins?

Yeah.

The kitchen door slammed open.

Glen, goddammit! It was Uncle Ralph.

Shit, said Glen.

Get inside!

We slouched back to the house. In the kitchen Uncle Ralph muttered something rough to Glen. To me he said this was Canada, Ernie, and I'd catch a damn cold without a coat on.

In the smoky parlour it was still only my mother's voice speaking. She was ending her camp stories—she'd tell them more, she said, another time. But then, as some in the room were making getting-up moves, and Gramma was yawning, our mother started talking about our father, though no one had asked, and said that yes, John, too, was really fine, and he had a

wonderful government job, but there was a revolution going on.
Did they know about the revolution? Well, there was a revolution. And because of the revolution John couldn't send
money—so, that's why Papa paid the way over. A loan, of course.
John's last letter said things would soon calm down and then
he'd send money. It was just *hard right* now getting money out,
really, because of the fighting . . . but the family wasn't listening
as closely any more. I shot her a look. Gramma yawned again.
The visit had lasted over an hour. She should stop—she could
tell about our father some other time, too. And she did stop.
And her family crowded into the front hallway and shrugged on
coats and tugged on boots and trooped out past Grampa at his
open door gravely saying "Farewell" to each; a little joke. From
the porch, their breath showing, they called, not loud because
of the neighbours, "Nice to see you!" "We'll see you!" "See you
soon!" Except Uncle Ralph. He waited until he was on the sidewalk by his car, and then he shouted, "Don't take any wooden
nickels!" Glen probably shot him a look.

Just before bed, in Uncle Alfred's old room, Jerry's now, we
went over the day. Our mother didn't seem to want the day to
end; as Jerry and I sat on his bed, she took small steps this way
and that. She could've "talked till dawn" downstairs, she said.
She had so much to tell them—and they were so interested,
weren't they? Think of it, boys, this was now home, *home*! Our
own rooms! No more suitcases! Turkey! A sleigh! Lovely, lovely!
She was mixing up Dutch and English, saying whatever word or
sentence jumped out first. How long had she been doing that?
I suppose it could be funny if both languages were understood
but if not—eyes would glaze over; Gramma's lips stiffen.

And hadn't she been right, our mother asked, about her
family? Characters, sure, but weren't they nice? Wasn't Grampa

smart? Uncle Ralph funny? Wait for Aunty Ada's strawberry shortcake! This was a new beginning, boys! Like Daddy wanted. Like she wanted. The day after tomorrow we'd start school— yes, she'd arranged it by letter from London. Jerry smiled. I think he was looking forward to school. Yes, she said, everything, boys, would be just "damn fantastic!" But before she kissed our foreheads good night, she stood at Jerry's window looking out on her old dark street. "Earrings," she murmured. It must have been a private thought-out-loud.

Much later I heard Grampa and Gramma coming upstairs, heard their door shut. Would Glen have liked my London stick? Would the stick have looked good with draped gabardine pants?

The first day of school, the third in Toronto, was amazing. My mother, but especially my father, had endlessly insisted— starting the first day out of camp!—on how important, how necessary school was. I'd have to work hard, yes, to "catch up," but it would be so interesting, so enjoyable. It would be boring at best, I was certain, and probably awful; also, school was surely connected with "discipline," one of my father's favourite words. So I was nervous that morning, not happy. Find the Boys Entrance, my mother said, and then the Office: I was expected. Should she come along? Please *no*. A three-minute trot from Osborne Avenue, Kimberley Public School was a two-storey red-brick massive block of a building with tall wide windows and all around a fenced-in yard of crushed cinder—already filled with hundreds of running, shrieking children. I'd never seen so many together! Eyes down, I marched through them in the short-pants English-boy suit and Hubie's extra-polished riding boots—my best outfit. A man holding a bell guarded the Boys

Entrance. Up the stairs and to the right I'd see the Office sign, he said. Wide wooden stairs, worn to a slope in the centre, not so clean—and then the smell hit me. A strange wonderful smell. I sucked it in. I'd discover it was made up of many different smells: ink, glue, wood, carbolic soap, wood oils, piss, wet wool, paint, dust, fresh sweat, stale sweat, soured milk, old food, running shoes. It was the smell of school.

A woman in a long-sleeved dark-brown dress waited in the Office—tall with a large high bosom, a head full of small brown curls, brown eyes swimming huge behind rimless glasses, and a tiny mouth. *She* was *Miss Tock,* my *teacher,* she said smiling, and I was in *Grade Six.* She spoke very clearly in a soft voice; I would never hear her raise it. *We* should go to class *before* the *bell* and find *me* a *good seat, all right?*

Yep, I said.

Not speaking, we climbed more stairs, walked down an empty hardwood-floor hall, footsteps clopping, and turned into a high-ceilinged room crowded with rows of one-piece wooden desk seats. In the back was an alcove where I had to hang up my coat. Miss Tock pointed to the second seat of the centre row that faced her desk. She turned to the blackboard behind her, wiped off other writing with her left hand, and in red chalk wrote ERNEST HILLEN with her right; her hands were as small as a girl's. I looked around me. Thirty desks at least, and the walls, and also the lower halves of the windows, jammed with drawings, paintings, cut-outs, photographs of animals and flowers, mountains and waterfalls, the largest map I'd ever seen, of Canada, and in a corner on top of a cupboard a globe—I knew about globes!—and a large grey stuffed bird. A bell rang faintly outside and then a roaring wave of shrill voices and thumps and clatter surged up stairs and bowled down halls. I stared hard at the top of my desk; a lidded inkwell sat in a hole in the upper right-hand corner. Kids came stomping into the room, breathing hard, flopped down with groans; not speaking, though. In a moment it grew still. I felt the eyes on me, kept my head down. The desk's surface was a blur of inked and carved doodles and of hearts, arrows, numbers, initials, and, in capital letters, the word PRICK.

In front of me I heard a light tapping, and I *had* to look up. Miss Tock stood behind her desk holding a ruler. Kids were rising around me, stepping out of their desks to the right. I did, too. Roll-call? *Bowing?*

Miss Tock tapped her desk again.

"God save our gracious King," she began to sing and the class at once joined in. I knew that song. British soldiers bellowed it. The children sang as if they'd sung it many times before. I hummed along, eyes on Miss Tock. "God save the King!" it ended.

Miss Tock put the ruler on her desk, clasped her hands in front of her, lowered her head.

"Our Father who art in Heaven," she began and the class joined in. A prayer. I dropped my head, too. I was pretty sure I'd heard the prayer before, in Dutch. Was this done every day in school, singing and praying?

"Amen."

The children quietly slid into their seats. Me, too.

Miss Tock didn't sit down. She pointed to the blackboard and then, smiling at me, said my name. In her clear way, she said *Ernest* had *just* arrived in Canada, and he was *Dutch*.

I watched her little mouth.

This was Ernest's *first* day in school, and *lucky* for *them* he'd be in *their* class! *Welcome Ernest!*

Welcome Ernest, the class muttered.

If you were *Dutch,* Miss Tock said, that *usually* meant you came from *Holland.* Did anyone *know* where Holland *was*?

A hand was raised to my left.

Yes?

A girl stepped out of her desk.

Europe, Miss Tock.

Correct.

The girl sat down.

But *Ernest,* Miss Tock said, did *not* come to Canada from Holland. *He* came from a country that *belonged* to Holland—what was called a *colony*—and *that* country was named the *Dutch East Indies.* Had anyone heard of the *Dutch East Indies*?

No hands.

It was a *country* made up of *thousands* of *islands,* and Ernest came from the *island* of *Java.* Who had heard of *Java*?

No hands.

I felt two light pats on my back, like a "hello." I didn't turn around.

Well, said Miss Tock, Java was *almost* on the *other side* of the *world* and they'd learn about it *later.* Because of the *war,* she said, Ernest had *missed* a *bit* of *schooling,* but *she* thought he would *fit* just *fine* in Grade Six. Didn't *Ernest* think so, *too*?

Yep, I said. I still felt all those eyes, but it was interesting, talking about me.

Ernest had been *speaking English* only for a *short while,* said Miss Tock, so *he* was still *learning* it. But then *none of you,* she said looking around the class, can speak *Dutch, can* you?

It was a little joke.

Was there *anything* she'd said *so far,* she asked me smiling, that I had *not understood?*

Nope, I said.

Learning a *new language* is *hard work,* said Miss Tock, *especially* if *everybody* around you knows *only that* language and you can't use *your* language. Does anyone *here* speak *another* language?

The hand of the boy in front of me flew up.

Miss Tock nodded at him.

The boy stepped out of his seat.

His father knew French, Miss Tock.

Thank you.

The boy sat down.

From *now on,* Miss Tock said looking at me, smiling again, I could *put up my hand*—as I'd *seen* the *others* do—and tell her at *any time* if I did *not* understand something. Would I *promise* to *do* that?

Yep, I said, smiling back at her. Clearly Miss Tock liked me. Well, I liked her, too.

The brown eyes rested on me, patiently swimming, the small mouth went on smiling. It was very still.

Holy shit! I suddenly understood—and shot out of my desk.

"Yes, Miss Tock," I said, standing straight.

"*Thank you,* Ernest," she said.

Another friendly pat on my back.

Miss Tock said the class was going to read now, and I could just sit and listen; next time I'd have my own book. Kids rummaged in their desk drawers. Mine was empty.

Miss Tock called a child's name, and he or she would read out loud standing up until Miss Tock said thank you, said another name, and then that kid would read.

The bell rang. Books were tossed back inside the desks. Children rose. A hand on my shoulder turned me around: it was the patter. An open, friendly face, blue eyes, neatly combed shiny wavy blond hair the colour of Hubie's, golden.

C'mon! he said, and taking my elbow tugged me towards the door. I looked at Miss Tock, but she was talking to a girl.

It was okay, the boy said. Recess.

What, I wondered, was "recess?" Coat? I asked.

Nah, said the boy.

In the hallway we plunged into a river of hurrying kids, boys and girls, little ones, big ones, all talking, all making fast for the stairs; no running, though. The blond boy concentrated on slipping past those ahead, taking the stairs sometimes three at a time; I could do that.

Outside the Boys Entrance he stopped.

He was Ronald Glenesk, he said, squinting in the sudden bright daylight. What about baseball?

Yep. I said.

Had I played it?

Nope.

Had I *seen* it played?

Nope.

Never mind, he said, c'mon! and started running to the far side of the yard; I tried to keep up. Other boys our size were hurrying in the same direction. And then I lost Ronnie and I was alone in the middle of a loudly squabbling group of about twenty. One or two slapped me on the back, another on my arm. Friendly? Were they friendly slaps? They wore long pants, jackets with zippers, running shoes, and there was I in a pale-grey short-pants suit and riding boots. Oh God—I'd have to fight! No choice. No escape. I'd known it since I woke up: new boys always had to fight. All over the world—that's how it was. I balled my fists. Leather boots at least, against running shoes.

All the dim days in camp, new boys had to fight, dizzy or not dizzy, sores or no sores—the rule of the tough; my rule, too. You didn't like fighting? Too bad. Scared? Too bad. Did I still know *how*? God, I hadn't fought for six, seven months, not since before Hubie . . .

Same team, Ernie! said a smiling Ronnie, suddenly beside me again. C'mon! and he jogged over to the corner of the yard's fence. Some boys quickly fanned out facing the corner; three of them busily scuffed up small mounds of cinders. Ronnie pointed to the mounds and, speaking fast, said that was First Base, that Second Base, that Third, and this was Home, where we were standing. His face was red, from running, from the cold. Someone handed him a bat. He passed it to me. I was First At Bat, he said, because I was the new guy. This was how I should grip it and swing it—and he showed me. The kid straight ahead holding the ball, he was the Pitcher. He'd throw the ball and I had to hit it and then run like hell to First Base. That was all for now. Three swings, okay?

Okay.

Ronnie joined a bunch of boys to the side, leaving me alone clutching the bat, except for a kid squatting behind me. I could feel a lot of eyes.

Play ball! Play ball! voices yelled.

I watched the Pitcher. A tall boy, he first twisted his body oddly and then threw the ball—but much too fast. I swung anyway, and almost fell over.

The squatter caught it though, and tossed it back to the Pitcher.

Nice swing, Ernie! Ronnie shouted. And others did, too— Nice swing, Ernie!

The Pitcher swivelled and threw the ball. Too fast again. I swung hard, but stayed on my feet. On whose side was the Pitcher?

Way to go, Ernie!

Way to go!

Nice try!

The squatter returned the ball. Whose side was *he* on?

This time the Pitcher swung himself half around and threw the ball—like a bullet. Not a ball that could be hit.

Strike three! somebody called. I laid the bat down. There was then some disagreement in Ronnie's group. Strange game: so far the only people who'd played were the Pitcher and me, and the squatter, I supposed. Everybody else, the boys fanned out in front and the ones to the side, just stood around. And then a voice from the side yelled:

"Give 'im another chance!"

Yeah! came a second voice.

Another chance! from a third.

Some of the boys in front of me were then shouting it, too. Weren't they the enemy?

Another chance!

Another chance!

Give 'im another chance!

In the wintry sunshine it was like a chant.

Ronnie ambled over, grinning, and said I was still At Bat. I could try a few more hits.

The Pitcher then didn't do his body trick, he just lobbed the ball over, and I almost hit it.

Attaboy, Ernie!

Attaboy!

Attaboy!

Shouts and yells from all over. No question, I was getting the hang of it.

The Pitcher tossed again, and I felt sure the bat touched the ball, though the ball didn't change direction.

Close one, Ernie!

Close, close, close!

The next ball came at me like a kiss, in the sweetest, slowest way, just reaching for the bat—and I *whacked* it. It rolled in a fine straight line to the Pitcher.

And there was shouting! There was cheering. There was hand-clapping. The boy on First Base jumped up and down. I got the craziest feeling and clamped down my jaws. It was just as if I was going to cry.

Nice hit, Ernie!

Way to go!

Attaboy!

C'mon! Another one!

And I did. I hit that ball several more times. The Pitcher kept throwing, I kept swinging, the squatter kept catching, and then the bell rang.

Nice going! said Ronnie as we trotted back to the Boys Entrance. Inside the school I breathed in the smell.

When the lunch bell rang I ran home fast. There was a lot to tell; my mother would have questions. Over Campbell's tomato soup and a grilled cheese sandwich in the kitchen, I reported on the *thousands* of kids in the yard, the smell, the noise, Miss Tock, Grade Six, the gashed desk, Ronnie, and baseball. Gramma was home, and listened along. I noticed then that the fruit bowl on top of the icebox still held no fruit. What had my mother and Gramma done that morning, I asked, as a polite child would. They'd been shopping, my mother said, and she'd discovered that, like in London, they'd had some rationing in Canada, too, sugar, butter. If they'd gone shopping, I thought, where was the fruit? On our first day the bowl had been full, grapes and bananas dangling over the side. Jerry and I had stared at it and Gramma had said go ahead take a piece "any time you feel like it." She couldn't have known it, but to us, then, abundance *plus* getability of food was still sort of paradise. To us, that invitation said much more about how pleased our grand parents must be to have us there than private rooms, presents, turkey dinners, or Christmas trees—no one had ever been so generous. We took Gramma at her word, though in time I know we would've calmed down. Anyhow, by the middle of the second day the bowl was empty. But now it was the middle of the third day and still no fruit.

There came a moment when Gramma left to sit in the parlour. Tell Gramma to buy fruit, I said to my mother. No, she couldn't tell Gramma to buy anything, wouldn't even ask her. Gramma and Grampa were doing enough for us; plenty! Yes, she knew we'd been told we could take without asking, but we'd damn well overdone it. She should've seen it coming, of course. *But*, from *now on*, she said, *when* Gramma bought *fruit*, we could take *only one* piece *each* a *day*—unless *offered* more. Was that *understood*? She sounded like Miss Tock. And we *must never ever* take the *last* piece. She had more to say, she said, but she'd wait until Jerry got home.

I walked softly upstairs (already routine), and changed clothes. Clothes, Glen had said, were important. I'd seldom wear Hubie's boots again, the English-schoolboy suit never. Words were important, too: from now on more yeahs and nahs than yeps and nopes. I was making a decision pulling on slobby long pants. Glen I wanted to *be*, sure, but that would take time;

I'd only see him again next Sunday when we were invited for supper. Meanwhile, I was going to be like the boys at school, not different, not special. Pinocchio wanted to be an ordinary boy, and so did I. The last time I'd been just another normal kid was in camp, after that, right up until, hell, that morning in class, I'd been special. No more! The plantation, the camps, pain-and-death, the *Devonshire*, London, all that was really of no *use* here. So forget it. Start over. Become *un*special—fast. I'd concentrate on it—all the hours at school. Watch Ronnie. Watch everybody. Watch and listen and learn. I would *fit* in *fine*, Miss Tock had said. Damn right!

And I had help. That same afternoon during recess—fast balls, three misses, out. And I was glad, though "Give 'im another chance!" echoed, of course, forever. To Miss Tock that afternoon, and from then on, I was just another student, a slow one maybe, *one* who had *missed* a *bit* of *schooling*. Nodding at my trousers, Ronnie said that was better. From him I'd learn the most. Baseball's strange dos and don'ts, the ways of school, Canadian English, how to get an after-school job, and the grown-up kindness and courtesy he showed his mom who was raising him and his brother alone while working at Eaton's selling lingerie. Ronnie was an excellent guide.

That night upstairs, for the first time since early on in the war, our mother talked seriously about rules. Such talks had always been discussions; not this one. First Jerry had to hear about the fruit, of course. Then she said that she'd been asked that we three use the kitchen door from now on, not the front door, and to, please please, shut the lights off after us. Bedtime for me was eight on weekdays, nine on Saturdays: I was a schoolboy now. Jerry's hours would vary because he was older and had a lot of homework. We shouldn't for a while hang up pictures in our rooms. All food was Gramma's business: no peeking in the icebox or cupboards. Money was a problem. Daddy couldn't send any yet. She wanted to work, to teach in a public school, but Grampa had said no. He didn't want Gramma to have to look after us—which mostly just meant fixing me a lunch; Jerry ate at Malvern Collegiate—so our mother had to stay home. We should try and find after-school jobs and, by the way, such jobs could be fun, and we'd get to keep some of what we earned as our first real pocket-money! And please, we should bother Grampa as little as possible: he was tired most days. He'd told her, she said to me, smiling a little at last, "Ernest can talk a bird out of a tree." Didn't he always have a special funny way of saying things? Had she ever told us what Grampa used to say when she and Ada and Alfred and dead sister Helen were young? The strongest, most critical word I had ever heard her voice about anyone in her family, and very rarely at that, was "goofy." Now she said, still smiling, "Goofy Papa would say, 'Children are a necessary evil.'"

FIVE / A Normal Boy

BY THE FOURTH DAY IN TORONTO, the second of school, I felt I'd begun, as was promised, to live "normally." It took the first three days, I suppose, to unlearn waiting for the promise to come true. My mother always kept her word, but it could take a while. In camp she'd vowed that I would see my father again and, sure, three and a half years later, that came true. In Batavia she'd said I would live "normally" in Toronto, Canada, and, sure, here I was, four months later. The absence of waiting for a promise to come true felt very restful. It wouldn't last long, but for a time in Toronto all that mattered was Now.

And Now, of course, meant normal life in a real home and in school. Our arrival in the Watson household had slightly loosened routines, but these, by the fourth day, were firmly back in place. They weren't complicated. We needed simply to remember that Grampa was King and Gramma was Queen. The King's job was to be King. The Queen's job was to keep the King content. The Queen had done a very good job for a long time, and that was just as well for us, but perhaps also for her: in the King's own words, if something, whatever, was off, "there'd be hell to pay." Though he was a quiet man who preferred reading to talking, the King was not a shy man and, if he wasn't happy, he'd let you know. But he was a man of regular habits so that, if nothing and no one interfered with these, of which the Queen tried to make sure, all was well. The best thing really, we learned quickly, was to stay out of sight and hearing when he was leaving for or returning from work, reading, listening to the radio, eating supper, telephoning, sleeping, or on his way to the bathroom. This didn't mean we never saw or talked to him; we did. But it was wise then to go through Gramma or our mother, as in, "I'd like to tell Grampa something," so they could pick the right moment. I don't know how he was with friends, or if he had any, but in our time under his roof the rare visitors were relatives only and with us he was always inside his "fine little sense of humour"—an invisible, very tough balloon no one could puncture to see who he was. Well, actually, I caught a glimpse once, but that was when we'd already been in Canada a couple of months.

In school, by the fourth day, the watch-and-listen plan was in full operation and, little dumb head buzzing, I felt I was learning by the hour. It couldn't go fast enough, though, becoming an ordinary boy! In class the old "all-ears" look fooled and pleased Miss Tock, but it was what kids said and did that was important—everyday language, opinions, and jokes; gestures, postures, and faces pulled; ways of teasing, praising, and insulting (and how to make one mean the other). Kids were the teachers and one day I wanted it to show in their eyes—in everybody's eyes—that I was just one of them, no different. What helped enormously were movies, comics, and radio. With Gramma treating Jerry and me that first week, "going to the show"—always a double bill—quickly became for me a weekly must, with ticket money scrounged up somehow. Stories and characters faded, but not the trademark moves and mannerisms of the stars, electric presences all, who, in just a few weeks, strode into my life in seven-mile boots—Errol Flynn, John

Wayne, Humphrey Bogart, Tyrone Power, Alan Ladd (my father's double), James Cagney, Hopalong Cassidy, The Marx Brothers, Cary Grant, Gary Cooper, and even Jimmy Durante. For a few hours in the dark, I adventured and loved along with them— *became* them. Afterwards there was a vast choice of piercing eyes, snarls, grins, twitches, salutes, drawls, and walks to practise privately in front of mirrors, to briefly make my own and then discard again. It was easy to tell that just about all boys in school did that—and girls, too—and so we had at least that language of mimicry in common. And then there were the comics where, already Tarzan's good friend, I met up within days, during recess and after school, with *The Lone Ranger, Little Orphan Annie, Popeye, Superman, Archie, Mandrake the Magician, King of the Royal Mounted,* and so on. The "language" of action drawings and words inside little clouds I soon grasped. Radio took longer because of house rules.

Normal living also included supper at the Holways that first Sunday and about once a month after that. Their home, modest beside the others on Pine Glen Road, was about a mile's walk south from the flat land around Osborne Avenue, across Kingston Road, into the heart of a suddenly hilly enclave of curving quiet streets, tall trees, large cared-for houses, and two small ravines, one deep and all bush, the other shallow and all grass; Pine Glen ran steeply down and ended at an old wooden bridge that crossed the shallow one.

Eyes twinkling, Uncle Ralph in a yellow sweater swung wide the glass front door—"Swell that you're here!" The bright smoke-filled living room already held other guests, as it often would, usually people just in for a drink, relatives (his), neighbours, or customers (he owned a factory that made paper boxes). A restless and noisy host, Uncle Ralph pressed drinks, told funny stories, never sat down. He liked guests to be cheery, as he was, and would grow more so as the evening wore on until he'd pace about playing snatches of songs on his violin and be so pleased if anyone sang along. Quiet Aunty Ada and Shirley Ann served cocktail snacks but mostly laboured in the kitchen. Glen didn't show himself and, if he was home at all, I'd have to ferret him out in his tiny foul room behind the kitchen; an upstairs bedroom was rented to a college student.

Our mother was introduced, as she often would be, as Anna, the sister-in-law . . . "she was a Jap prisoner, you know." This usually silenced the room. What to say? Gees and goshes. But then there might be someone who, like Uncle Alfred, would ask, "How bad was it?" Our mother learned, over time, as did Jerry and I, to evade both the question and the sudden awkward attention with an airy "We survived *fine*" or "It could've been *worse*" and was seldom pressed for much more. People were polite, certainly, but not really interested. This sometimes baffled Jerry and me—on the *Devonshire*, in London, now in Toronto. Were they just dumb, or what? She'd always respond, a little defensively, that, no, no, it wasn't that, it was simply, well, *difficult* for people to understand what they hadn't experienced, and they had no idea, and never would have, and don't worry about it. So at Uncle Ralph's that afternoon she told one or two short mild stories and then went "to help Ada."

Conversation resumed. The Holway home would be really the only one where I'd hear adults conversing; we weren't asked out much—our mother's old friends had married and scattered. That first visit, Jerry and I drank Cokes, and I sat still and listened for a few minutes until I felt I could decently leave to hunt up Glen. And so it would be on other Sundays—for a short while I'd pick up fragments of grown-up talk on topics which grew familiar from repetition. The topics were lawn-care, money, cottages, a game called golf, liquor brands, Jews, cars, illnesses, fishing, road conditions, the Depression, paint, foreigners, the prices of things, City Hall, teenagers, life insurance, fur coats, rationed tires, salesmanship, food, new tools, hockey, the weather of course, but not the war, never the war; you wouldn't know it had happened.

Aunty Ada's suppers were feasts for us. Her dining-room table blinked with crystal and silver and steamed with dishes complementing roast chicken or well-done roast beef. In the centre always sat a large glass plate on which, on a carpet of iceberg lettuce, she had arranged, in precise circles, straight lines, and turrets, sliced tomatoes and cucumbers, thin celery sticks, green olives, sweet gherkins, and sculpted radishes. You didn't have to ask, she said, you could reach out and eat from it the whole meal through—after the fruit-bowl fiasco, Jerry and I took it slow. The crowning touch was usually her famous strawberry shortcake, so fine it was, as my father might've said, "as if angels peed on your tongue." Holway strife, if there was any, and certainly father and son collided sometimes, was put on hold. At the head of the table, Uncle Ralph would have the most to say, cheery banter mainly that included all. Aunty Ada stuck to gently urging everyone to eat more; Glen and Jerry always did her proudest. Shirley Ann said little but could react with sudden sweetly pealing laughs. For a few hours in her sister's house my mother would glow almost like she had on the ship.

After that first supper, as would become routine, Glen and I took off fast with Patchy—a man's gotta have his smoke! Except for one or two other muffled-up dog-walkers, the sparsely lit streets were deserted; clouds hung thick in the darkness overhead. Alone, our age difference had fallen away again, and I was as pleased to be with Glen as I'd been in Grampa's backyard. He let me try rolling one myself and we lit up at the top of the wooden stairs to the bridge, the shallow ravine below us black as an ocean.

Did I do push-ups? he asked.

We clumped to the bottom of the stairs.

What were push-ups?

Glen handed me his cigarette and Patchy's leash and let himself drop forward flat down on the bridge. Then slowly, his weight on the tips of his fingers and on his toes, body stretched rigid, he pressed himself up until his arms were straight, slowly came down again until his nose touched the bridge, up again slowly—ten times he did that and stood up not the least out of breath.

Those were push-ups, he said, taking back his smoke and Patchy. One of the best goddamn all-around exercises. He did fifty a day, twenty-five on finger tips. If the mood hit him, twice a day. A man had to stay in shape. Staying in shape was the thing, Ernie. Let him see me do some.

I gave Glen my cigarette to hold and got down on all fours. It had looked easy. I leaned forward on my fingertips but they promptly collapsed.

Use your whole hand, Glen instructed.

I stretched out, then pressed up hard, but, as head and shoulders lifted slightly, the rest didn't budge.

Keep your toes together.

I pushed up as hard as I could, and head and shoulders and calves rose a bit, but not the ass. So I stuck up my ass.

Hands closer in.

I kept pressing, kept straining to wrench that heavy useless stupid body off the floor of the bridge. Parts of it obeyed, but never the whole. Couldn't I do just *one*? My arms were starting to hurt.

Well, I was sure getting there, Glen at last said kindly, freeing me to climb to my feet, a dizzy weakling, white spots dancing.

Practice. I needed practice, Glen said. Muscles were god-damn important.

I nodded. He was right. Absolutely.

Not white spots . . . snow flakes! Snow was falling! It was *snowing*! Flakes drifted down, melting at once as if shy, wetting my coat, Glen's coat, his hair, the bridge. White Halifax, endless white land from the train, now I was *inside* snow! White filled the darkness around us, more and more of it, blurring the end of the bridge, and then, not melting any more, the flakes sound-lessly piled one on top of the other, smelling like cold water.

It was snowing! I said.

Yeah, sure.

Muscles, Glen went on, you needed them. Tonight at Grampa's, I should try push-ups again, and tomorrow morning, and after school, and tomorrow night. He bet I'd do a couple by then. Maybe five or even eight by Friday. Twenty in a month, no sweat. Push-ups, push-ups, push-ups. And once started, I must never let up.

We wandered on in the new snow, not seeing a soul until we reached Queen Street. Glen talked and he had my full atten-tion. I watched his walk and loped along, hands deep in pockets. What I understood him to say was that the sure high purpose behind push-ups and other exercises, and behind sports, too, was that they led to "staying in shape." That is what you strove for, that was the end result. And a man had to stay in shape for two reasons: "getting girls" and "independence."

Girls, of course, were good for a man. Girls—well, where the hell would we be without girls? They made everything right. And girls loved muscles. That was just a fact: they liked looking at them and they liked feeling them. So, you needed muscles especially in summer on the beach, and you needed them when dancing and necking.

What was necking? I asked.

Serious kissing, was the meagre answer.

In time Glen would certainly shed more light on necking— probably drawing on some experience of what to do before and during and, drawing on his hopes and dreams, I think, of what to do next. We'd discuss in detail that sea of wondrous maddening mystery from which "necking" had bobbed up. But on our first walk he didn't stray far from push-ups.

Glen's other truth was that staying in shape was vital to gaining independence, as he put it, "to breathing free." To him that meant, first of all, "getting the hell out of the house." But it was more. His plan, and I felt it was something fairly private I was hearing, was to become a farmer. To become a farmer, he said, had been his plan for years. Jesus! my Canadian cousin had actually *tended a plan for years*! Glen had figured out that, besides enjoying the out-of-doors life which he, Glen, loved, only a farmer could be an entirely "self-sufficient" man. That was at the heart of it: only the self-sufficient man could be truly independent. What a farmer needed to live he could grow and build himself, unlike city people, unlike, for example, Glen's "old man." But farming was very hard work; you needed muscles, stamina; you had to stay in shape. Push-ups, Ernie.

We'd come to Queen Street. More lights, a few hurrying people, a streetcar, the shops all dark, except the one on the corner of Wineva where Glen treated me to my first milkshake, vanilla. Then we wandered back to his house.

Later, about half-past eight, my mother, Jerry, and I trudged back up the silent winding streets, across Kingston Road, to Osborne Avenue. It was still coming down so my brother and I stopped for a snowball fight, and our mother joined in. Hadn't it been a wonderful visit? she wanted to know. Wasn't everybody nice? The food delicious? And so much of it! The house *gezellig*? Uncle Ralph funny? Aunty Ada dear? Jerry and I agreed whole-heartedly. Jerry, I think, acquired the beginnings of a quiet crush on Shirley Ann that evening. Our mother was relentless, though, in expressing pleasure and gratitude, never failed to have these hadn't-it-been-great sessions on the way home from the Holways. And why not? They were our kindest and only hosts.

All that week I did push-ups, morning, noon, and night. And Glen was right: by Friday evening I did five, though not as slowly as he did, and never on fingertips. Within six weeks I'd worked up to twenty-five. The idea of push-ups to gain independence I hadn't entirely grasped yet, but push-ups to get girls made instant sense.

Ending with the five push-ups, that whole Friday had been a good day. Though already April, it had snowed twice more, wet stuff a foot high, so in Grampa's yard huge balls had been rolled and a fortress built. But most of all, it had been my birthday, the twelfth. At the beginning of the week my mother had suggested I make a wish list she'd pass around, and not to expect too much. I'd never written one before and thought it best to be reasonable and to give lots of choice.

Burth-list
1. a Dog.
2. a Bibe gun with 500 bullets.
3. a Stampablem.
4. a Long pair of trouzes.
5. a Jecked with a zipper.
6. a very long and strong piese of rope with a sharp nife, PLAESE will you.
7. a Rugbiball.
8. a bow and arrow's.
9. a Expreswagon, with 4 wiels.
10. a Tent, with a bed, and everything.
10. a pair of boxglows.
11. a Good pair of mocasins of leder.
12. a Pair of bedslippers.
13. a baisebel secondhand.
14. a pesket with al kainds of frood.
14. 6 tints with tomatejijce.
15. a very nais small kano.

Friday morning I had to open presents extra early, still in pyjamas, or Grampa'd be off to the office. My mother had decorated a chair at the kitchen table with coloured paper; packages and cards were piled on the seat. My brother and mother and Grampa and Gramma watched as I unwrapped trousers, a jacket with a zipper, a beginner's stamp album, six medium-size cans of tomato juice, a twenty-foot-long piece of rope, and a nine-inch-long knife in a leather sheath. I was extremely pleased. I thanked all four, though I didn't know who had given me what.

Why did I want a rope? Gramma asked. Everyone had wondered. Anna had just said, Go ahead, buy it: Ralph was giving the knife.

Wait, please, I said. I grabbed the rope and knife and ran, this once, upstairs. Two minutes later I was back in bathing trunks, knife stuck in the waist, coiled rope in hand. Gramma gaped at me. I opened the kitchen door and stepped into the grey snow of dawn. At great speed then, dodging spears, arrows, and bullets, I sprinted to the rear of the yard to a frozen maple tree with a thick branch jutting outward. In my room I'd already fixed a quick lasso knot on one end of the rope, slightly weighting it. That end I now flung with great strength and accuracy over the branch, caught it in powerful hands as it came down, punched the other end through the knot, and then yanked the rope fiercely hard so the knot raced up to grasp the branch. An easy action, practised a thousand pretend times on London's gargoyles, chimneys, and trees. I snatched out my killing knife, leapt panther-like onto the rope and, bare feet gripping it, swung back and forth, muscles rippling, calling the savage hunting cry of the bull ape that chilled the hearts of man and beast.

Goddammit! Get in the house! rasped Grampa from the kitchen doorway where the others had crowded in with him. I hopped back through the suddenly cold snow. Inside, my mother wrapped me in her brown cardigan, and shooed me off to get washed and dressed. Was Grampa really mad? I couldn't tell. Grinning, Jerry mouthed, CRAZY BASTARD! Gramma stared at me, wagging her head, not smiling.

Before I left for school, my mother read me my father's birthday letter—I could never make out his handwriting myself. At twelve I wasn't a little boy any more, he wrote from Batavia, but the youngest of older boys. I should now work on growing up big *inside,* good in thought and deed; growing up big *outside* was fun but not so important. I should fight hateful feelings, avoid mean talk, care for those I loved, help people, do them favours. A boy scout was asked to perform one good deed a day, which was more than most did, but much less than the effort of a really fine human being. Surprisingly, he wrote that I should take the wholly good Jesus as example; I remembered clearly hearing him say once that the church was "nonsense." None of us, of course, he went on, could reach such perfection but, if we really did our best, we could go a fair distance. He hoped I would become a hardworking, honest, good human being, and make him proud of me. He ended that he was looking deep into my eyes and asking, Ernest, will you do your best to grow up *big*?

His letters always told me how and who to be, which was maybe a father's job. But in my answer, then, I said nothing about push-ups. When I let him know once how much I liked jazz, he replied that he, too, had enjoyed it as a youth, but really so much of it was trivial and filched from the great composers . . . true art came from suffering . . . Vincent van Gogh was hungry all his life. A lesson, sure: I didn't mention music again. I reported that Glen had taken me to my first dance (in his school's auditorium, a fantastic evening of borrowed, hoisted-high draped gabardine pants, big-band sound in the sweaty half-dark, and Glen urging me to *Have some guts!* Do it! Ask her! Just shuffle around. *Ask* her! and I did). My father responded that I was a little young for dances and girls; that could wait. But he was wrong: it could not wait; but I didn't write him that. Maybe I'd become a lumberjack or a trapper when I grew up, I wrote, and, from the other side of the world, came a longish plea to scrap both notions. Could I, for instance, ever expect a wife to live in the wilderness? Raise children there? But by then I wanted to be a cowboy or a crooner. Reading his letters to me, my mother sometimes stopped. Daddy was a wise good intelligent serious responsible man, she'd say, who loved me very much, remember that. Jerry knew our father a lot better, could figure out his handwriting, and read his letters in private.

When that Friday's morning-recess bell set off the stampede for the door, Miss Tock's small hand flapped me to stay. Ronnie Glenesk looked back—what had I done? Unreadable, Miss Tock stood by her desk until the class had emptied. Then she seated herself. It was suddenly so still.

Happy birthday, she said, eyes swimming.

I moved to stand up, was waved down.

Thank you, Miss Tock.

You are *twelve* today.

Yes, Miss Tock.

Well, *congratulations. That* was *quite* an *age.* She had *not* said *anything* in *class* because she wasn't *sure* if I would have *appreciated* that, *all* the *attention.* But *still, she* wanted to *wish me* all the *best.*

I watched her nice little mouth speak.

Thank you, Miss Tock.

She wanted *me* to *know* that *she* was *very pleased* with *how* I was *getting along* in *class.* She *knew* it wasn't *easy.* And *now—did* I get some *presents*?

A rope and a knife, Miss Tock.

Very good, she said, and I was sure that she knew exactly what the rope and knife were for. Maybe Miss Tock knew this because she understood me a little because she liked me, and not just me, all the kids in class, she really liked us; you could feel it. Maybe that was why her face and voice lingered with me long after most of the teachers who followed her had faded; those teachers had always seemed to have so much more on their minds than us.

Ronnie was waiting in the yard to hear what Miss Tock had wanted. I'd already been in trouble once that week: I'd joined some boys swinging from water pipes in the school basement. The principal himself caught us. A grey-haired, slow-moving man, he marched us upstairs to the Office muttering about rules and penalties. We were lined up and each boy in turn held out a hand, palm up flat, which the principal whacked three times with the strap, a stiff short belt. Just hard taps, really, but still goddamn punishment-*hitting* again. When he came to me he said I was excused because I didn't know the rules yet. Yes, I did, sir, I said. The principal looked at me. Did I want the strap? he asked. Yes, sir, I said, not out of bravery at all, or loyalty, but terrified to be seen being treated differently. So I got my three whops—and what raced around the school immediately was that the weird new kid had *asked* for the strap.

Just a happy-birthday from Miss Tock, I told Ronnie. Well, that was fine. Maybe he had a present for me, he said, a job. I'd asked Ronnie earlier about jobs because he seemed to know all the merchants on Main Street where he worked in a grocery store. Kimberley bordered on Main and, after school, he took me across into one of the two drugstores there. I was the Dutch friend he'd mentioned, he said to the druggist. As in class and in the yard I watched Ronnie carefully: now he was talking to an adult—polite, friendly, alert, steady-eyed, hands out of pockets, and something else, something grown-ups might not pick up on, "clean" was maybe the word; I thought he was a boy who had very few bad thoughts. The druggist said, yes, he could use help on Saturdays and if Ronnie, being in the "delivery business" himself, would fill me in, I could start tomorrow, Saturday, at fifteen cents an hour plus tips.

The big worry next day wasn't finding addresses (the druggist had a map), transacting cash-on-delivery orders, or in-store chores, it was learning to ride a bike. The druggist had shown us the heavy black one for delivery use and, luckily, hadn't asked if I could handle it—with honest Ronnie there, I probably wouldn't have lied. I hadn't been on a bike, though, since before the war when Jerry had given me his, the finest thing he owned, for my birthday and, crotch on crossbar, I'd just been able to reach the pedals. Now I was suddenly expected to zip around snowy city streets. So, wheeling the bike along, I ran a lot, and, when I did mount it in alleys, I fell a lot; the druggist must have thought he'd hired a very slow boy. Still, by noon I'd gotten the hang of it again. What took longer to master, what I don't think Ronnie could have filled me in on, was the core of the delivery business—upping tips. Tips were a nickel, a dime, or a rare quarter. Women usually answered doors and were experienced tippers: they tipped what they always tipped. The trick was to get them to tip a little more. Ringing a door bell, I'd remember Ronnie's open stance facing an adult and, after the first half-dozen deliveries, added to that something of my own—a single short pleasant comment about the weather, or her house, her garden, her dog, whatever. I could tell it was unexpected; sometimes it worked. My father worried when he heard about tipping. Wasn't that the first step towards bribery, he wrote, towards selling yourself?

Jerry, too, was taken on part-time, at a gas station. From then on we both always had jobs. From our earnings our mother handed back pocket change: she badly needed what we brought in. Weeks would turn into months and no money from Indonesia. Once or twice, I think, my father was able to pass on a little to her in a complicated way via Holland; Gramma and Aunty Ada might have tucked the odd five dollars into her purse.

And then all at once it was spring. That was Canada for you! No warning! Overnight Grampa's brown grass turned green, flowers poked up, trees fuzzed, and bird song woke us crazy early to new soft smells. Not only that, but the entire school was going to the circus. A rumour for weeks and then suddenly, like spring, a certainty. Miss Tock said that in Maple Leaf Gardens, the big hockey rink downtown, we'd be seated amongst Grade Eighters, to keep us in line—and my stomach gave a heave. This was excellent news, and about the circus, too. Jean was in Grade Eight, a tall lean girl, round-shouldered, with blueish skin and lank blonde hair that veiled her eyes like Veronica Lake's. Whenever I saw her, I felt her pulling, like a flame, and near her I was drymouthed, jittery. She lived at the far end of Osborne, in a small unpainted house, smoked on the street, and wore lipstick—she'd wipe it off before coming into the schoolyard, hunched in a brown cloth coat, and dab it on first thing leaving. Usually alone, sometimes she stood chatting with bigger guys; no flirting, no romping. I'd never seen her smile or heard her voice. Thin as she was, she walked like a woman, leaving it to the hips. Many times I followed her at a distance down our street, watched her unlock the door, enter, and the door close. I was a Grade Sixer and she didn't know I was alive. But in Maple Leaf Gardens, in a hodgepodge of Sixers and Eighters, well, who knew?

On the afternoon we assembled at the doors of the Gardens—many doors and at least three or four other schools of kids and nervous teachers—I couldn't spot her. Maybe she hadn't come. Maybe she was too grown-up for a circus. Men in grey uniforms guided us into and up a maze of stairs and corridors and when they showed us our seats we were at the top of that rumbling gigantic place. A sea of heads sloped down to a huge rounded stage filled with tall upright ladders, striped tents, steel cages, and wires and nets strung up high. On a small separate stage glittered brass instruments and musicians dressed in silver.

More kids pressing in behind us, our class scrambled to sit, and then I saw her, goddammit! Two rows ahead, empty seats on her left. Without thinking I barged forward, side-shuffled into her row, and plunked down beside her. Right beside her! She sat unmoving, hands loose in her lap on the folded coat, hair hiding her eyes; she was watching the stage, I supposed. A quick look at her and I shifted my eyes there, too. She could sit like that, like wood, the whole circus through, I didn't care. I was next to her, closer than I'd ever been. I could smell her, if I liked. If it wasn't for the damn noise, I could've heard her breathe. On the armrest between us we might touch. Who knew? It grew dark, the stage flared into light. The circus was starting—words blasting from loudspeakers, drumrolls, trumpets, and applause would shatter the air for at least two hours, but for me, it would all be a distant hum. She smelled faintly of perfume, or maybe it was shampoo, and of chewing gum and cigarette smoke, and a fourth scent, strong and salty, *herself!* I inhaled—a sort of wild smell. Far below on the bright stage clowns tumbled and women climbed vertical ropes. Her elbow was on the armrest. I put mine there, too, careful not to touch her. Nothing wrong with sharing it though. It was hot in Maple Leaf Gardens. I eased my elbow a quarter inch closer. Below, dogs leapt through burning hoops. A half-inch to go. No hurry. Okay now, a quarter-inch more. Don't pull away, *please!* Muscled men and women climbed the standing ladders. At the top they reached for ropes with bars and swung out high above the stage. The last quarter-inch . . . gently. And then our elbows touched, oh, like feathers. A surge of applause from the audience; I hadn't seen what for. My elbow was on fire. It was sweltering in Maple Leaf Gardens. Seals honked. She sat so very still in the near-darkness, folded into herself. Clowns wheeled something onto the stage—a big golden cannon. Tripping towards it, dainty and small, came a helmeted woman in a green jump suit and riding boots. She stopped, bowed in all directions: drums pounding, the clowns levered her boots first into the barrel. There was a great sighing hush. Freeze now, I warned my elbow, don't spoil it, don't move any more, stay, this is perfect.

Boom! thundered the cannon.

Jesus! said Jean, and her elbow bumped mine. A hoarse voice, husky, beautiful.

People stood up around us, cheering. Jean didn't, so I didn't. The woman was way at the other end of the stage, bowing helmetless, long red hair blazing. They'd *shot* her out of the bloody cannon! Was there a light pressing on my elbow? What would Glen have done? I pressed back a little.

Jesus! Jean said again, louder this time: she was impressed. Such a voice!

Chest thudding—it was now or never. For God's sake, in camp *I'd danced with adult women!* Just be natural. Don't squeak.

Hi, I said.

She turned, hooked away some hair, and one pale eye, maybe it was blue, looked at me. Her elbow stayed steady.

Oh, hi, Ernie.

Sweet Lord, she knew my name! My *name!* All I could do was smile, a very pleased, dumb smile. She smiled back, the smallest parting of the lips, and her hand flew to her mouth. Too late— the dim light had shown lovely lovely brown English teeth.

Great, huh? I said.

She nodded, her eye still on me.

I flattened my palms on my pants to dry. What else to say? I looked away, down to the stage—just tigers and lions now. Jean turned her face there, too. And so we sat in the brassy hum for minutes, or half an hour, our elbows welded—God knows what the circus was doing. I was hot and very satisfied. But no, not entirely. Her hands just lay there, slack in her lap as before. I took the deepest breath, an underwater-swimmer's breath, moved my right hand forward and lowered it on hers, very slowly so she could easily yank it away. But she didn't. I breathed out and let my hand rest. Was this happening? Yes! I was dizzy, my ribs hurt. I'd just jumped across some great depth. Her hand felt cold and small and, suddenly, also frail, so I wrapped my fingers around it, clasped it softly, and, wonder of wonders, her hand stirred, turned a little, and snuggled in. We sat like that through the rest of the circus. Women leapt on and off cantering horses. Men somersaulted on the high wire. Elephants, finally, swayed to a waltz, and then, as Maple Leaf Gardens lit up, lumbered single file off stage, each elephant's trunk grasping the tail of the one ahead.

Jean squeezed my hand, let go, rose quickly, and turned to the bigger kids on her right. I backed away, lost sight of her in the crowd, and joined my very young classmates. In the days to follow I tried to catch her eye but couldn't. I didn't have the nerve to go up and speak to her. What would I say? Hey, remember? At the circus? No, she was an unreachable Grade Eighter again, and that was okay—for a little while we'd been outside the real world, or maybe *inside* it. I watched out for her less though.

Toronto days grew longer and warmer. In class we drowsed. There was another Holway supper. Aunty Ada sent me to find a can of something in the basement where I gawked at Glen's sports gear lying around: skates, hockey sticks, bicycles, skis, boots, poles, sleds, baseballs, gloves, bats, weights, footballs, badminton rackets, and a home-made ping-pong table. On Saturdays I pedalled drugstore orders around. To please Grampa, and my mother who suggested it, I offered to regularly polish the laced boots he wore, and he said, Go to it, young fellow! He also had Jerry and me rake up winter debris, pull dandelions, and mow the lawn. Easy chores. What he said was that it was Gramma who liked the garden looking "spiffy." This, I thought, was a little trick of Grampa's and Gramma's always to say that it was the *other* who did or didn't want this or that. For example, sometimes I preferred, as Tarzan would have, to leave the house barefoot via my bedroom window, cross the porch roof, and slide down a pillar. Gramma caught me once and, thin-lipped, warned me never to do it again because *Grampa* would get really mad. Nah, I thought, Grampa was a man, he knew about climbing; *she* was mad. So, I just stopped doing it when Gramma was home. Then for two days not at all while the porch got painted. On the third day it was dry and, after school, after Gramma drove off to pick up Grampa downtown, I went up to my room and came down again my way, oh, for the hell of it. The three of us were as usual upstairs after supper, when Grampa called me down. The front door was open—it was still light—and he was on the porch, wide-legged, fists on his hips, looking at several definite smudges on the spotless pillar. He turned and glared at me, a cigar butt clamped in his mouth.

Goddamn you, he growled. Did you do this?

Yes, Grampa.

He took a big step towards me, cigar stub quivering, and grabbed me by the arm above the elbow. Jesus! was he strong! His fingers dug in. It hurt. He began to shake me.

Did *you* do this? his voice louder, and rising. I goddamn well want to know! Did you? Did you?

He was shaking me so hard I was losing my balance, flopping around, my arms, legs, my head, teeth clicking.

Did you? Did you? Did you?

Jesus! this was like the push game!

Yes, Grampa! I did! I did! I yelped.

His face was an inch from mine and white. Sour breath and spittle flared; the cigar stump trembled wildly so he bared his lips and bit down on it—and I got my flash of Grampa's teeth, perfect like Gramma's but brown brown brown. The shaking went on.

Did you goddamn *do* this, you goddamn whippersnapper! You nitwit!

My eyes caught twirling fragments of porch, trees, and lawn, and a strange useless thought shot through my head: Grampa had gone to *university*.

I did! I'll clean up! I'm sorry, Grampa!

Sorry be goddamned! Sorry shit! You idiot!

And then he started kicking me, cigar end flipping, holding my arm, shaking me, his polished boot kicking my rear end, the backs of my legs. I tried to pull out of reach but no chance.

I'm sorry, Grampa! I yelled.

I was close to crying.

The hell with sorry! he bawled, and, almost dancing, he kept on shaking me, kicking me. I'll teach you sorry! *This*'ll teach you sorry!

It was as if he hadn't heard me, and suddenly I was cooling off. Was it the word "teach"? Cooling off and thinking. *What* was he teaching me? I'd *said* I was sorry. Cooling off and heating up. This was punishment-*kicking*, Grampa! I'd seen that a hundred times, oh yes. Women in the dust. Boots into flesh. Inside my head I screamed, Not any more, Grampa! Not any more, you fucking stupid old bastard! And furiously I wrenched myself loose, and ran for the door.

Get the hell back here! Grampa roared.

I kept going, up the stairs, into my room, and slammed the door and locked it. Jerry knocked. What happened? I lay on my bed, panting, didn't answer. My mother knocked. Was I okay? Go ask Grampa! I shouted. And I think she did because I heard her go downstairs. I must have fallen asleep, because the next morning I couldn't remember hearing her come back. Before school, but after Grampa had left for work, I cleaned the pillar with one or two wipes of a wet cloth. There was no talk later about what happened. I didn't climb out of my window again. And I was more cautious with Grampa and Gramma: maybe they really just felt the same about things.

Summer hit as suddenly as spring, sometimes rising to marvellous Java-like heat and humidity. School closed, a relief, to be honest, after several months of it; many kids took off for camps or cottages. Jerry found a full-time summer job as an office boy and I a temporary one, via Aunty Ada who'd worked there once, making popsicles in a dairy off Main Street. After work and on weekends Jerry and I teamed up again—we'd grown apart some because of school—and roamed the Beach, saw movies. We only ate and slept in Gramma and Grampa's home: it wasn't ours. We were grateful to live there—as our mother so often said we should be—but it was a rooming house, like the brides' hostel, and that was okay, a home would come, she'd begun promising again, a home would come.

One hot early-July Sunday, Uncle Ralph drove his family and us to Niagara Falls. Very near the deafening, misty run-off, we panicked needlessly when Jerry disappeared over a little wall. Jerry, of course, never did anything stupid: there were many paths and walls still to go before the long steep drop into the boiling whirlpools. Later, somewhere on the side of a quiet road in tall grass we picnicked on crustless chicken sandwiches gone limp. Glen then lay back and stared up at the sky; next to him, I did the same. He folded his hands behind his head and sighed; I did too. Then he closed his eyes; I shut mine. On the way back I sat up front between Uncle Ralph and Aunty Ada and he and I sang one of his favourite violin tunes, "Deep in the Heart of Texas," and slapped the dashboard. While everyone dozed, Uncle Ralph whispered that he'd heard of a better job than popsicle-making, more fun and tips, by a lake where he'd sometimes fished. If it was okay with my mother, he'd drive me out next weekend. I'd love it, he said, and he meant that sincerely.

And I did. Every day for nearly two months I would bless my luck at being in that place, a place often so still no fish jumped unheard. The lodge on Rice Lake, twenty-some miles north of Cobourg—Boats, Fishing, Cabins, and Live Bait—was run by a

Mr. and Mrs. Donald. Big friendly sun-burnt people, they worked hard and swore a lot, he twice as much as she, and she five times more than my mother; you got used to it. The lodge's Big House, entirely fronted by a screened-in porch, sat right by the water and behind it stretched a lawn three times the size of Grampa's, then a vegetable garden in full sun, and behind that, in pine-tree shadow, a half-dozen one-room cabins Mr. Donald had built himself. Guests only slept there though; they ate, drank, and played darts, cards, table-tennis, piano, and gramophone records in the Big House. Besides several guest rooms, the Big House also held the lounge, dining room, kitchen, the Donalds' apartment, and my room, a tiny walled-off space at one end of the porch with its own door, open to the lake's every breeze and night-sound and a view from my bed of the Canadian moon and stars shimmering.

On the first day Mr. Donald strode about the grounds with me explaining my duties. I would be his and Mrs. Donald's personal "jack-of-all-Jesus-Christ-trades" but also have "full son-of-a-bitch responsibility" for some things. And sure, I was at his and Mrs. Donald's beck and call, but they both routinely helped out, as, amazingly, did some guests, and there was always time for sudden ice-cream runs to town, surprise fishing trips, and for, as he called it, just "goddamn horsing around." Mr. Donald knew what he was doing: he'd work me hard but never on tasks I couldn't handle and make fun—and in no time at all what happened was this: I felt like a part-owner. I was to take care of, he said, the boats (clean), tackle (sort), the garden (weed, water, harvest), the lawn (mow), eggs (gather), milk (fetch), the front porch (sweep), meals (help serve), and the guests ("Keep the bastards happy!"). But on my first day, I should do "bugger all." I could swim, but only with others around: the lake had fish as big as me and snapping turtles that could bite off a foot. He must have seen me eye his large tomato planting because he said I could eat as "bloody many" as I "bloody wanted."

We'd done the tour and were resting on the dock, his rubber-booted feet dangling in the water, when Mr. Donald gave me to keep the lodge's brochure with a long poem inside called "Fishing." This was what "we're goddammit-to-hell all about," he said, and read some of it, right there with tied-up boats softly thumping the dock and a hollow wet whispering underneath.

A feller isn't thinkin' mean,
Out Fishin'.
His thoughts are mostly good and clean;
Out Fishin'.

He doesn't knock his fellow men
Nor harbour any grudges then,
A feller's at his finest when,
Out Fishin'.

The rich are comrades of the poor;
All brothers of a common lure,
Out Fishin'.

The brothers of the rod and line
An' sky and stream are always fine;
Men come close to God's design,
Out Fishin'.

A feller isn't plotting schemes
Out Fishin'.

He's only busy with his dreams
Out Fishin'.

His livery's a coat of tan,
His creed to do the best he can;
A feller's mostly always man,
Out Fishin'.

I didn't go to sleep the first night—nor many of the nights to follow—until the Big House did. Just as it had grown still, I climbed out of bed again and knelt. I wasn't much for praying, the last time was years ago when I'd begged God to get me some lead soldiers, fast. On Rice Lake, though, I had no requests. If Jerry or my mother had been there we would've talked it out about the lake, the ducks, the rowboats and canoes, my swearing bosses, the thousands of ripening tomatoes, the outside hand-pump to wash under, the chickens, the guests, the huge lunch, the huge supper, my first tip (a silver American dollar), fishes that nosed my hand underwater, bulrushes, loons calling, Betty, frogs croaking, my room, and my personal oil lamp. As it was, I'd already scrawled a postcard to my mother but, after How are you? It's great here! Send my long brown pants! I'd run out of space. Somebody needed to be told though—the wind and the water and the pine trees insisted. The day's pleasure and beauty had stunned a little. How could such a wondrous lovely place be? It was almost not believable. I hadn't thought of them for months, but then I was suddenly sure that this perfect patch of Canada had to be loaded with Manang's spirits. It made complete sense for spirits to be hovering about here. So, what went up to God that night from the sleeping lodge was just a fairly detailed list of thank-yous. More such tallies rose that summer.

I thought I'd get homesick, but no. Work and "horsing around" filled all the hours, sometimes until midnight. By the end of the first day, I'd been made to feel like a member of the family, an extremely hospitable family with always a slew of friends staying over. Most guests were just that, friends, people who felt like part-owners, too, who frowned on change, who had travelled far, many from America, for their yearly dose of babying and bossing. The "bastards" didn't always know it, but like a loving uncle and aunt the Donalds remembered and slaved to indulge their littlest ways and wishes. That was expected of me as well and it was fun, actually, pampering strangers "behind their backs" and later boasting in the kitchen of having again secretly disentangled dumb Mrs. So-and-so's fishing line or that Cabin 4 unknowingly still downed double desserts every day. In the evening hosts and guests mixed in the lounge—just a big family playing games and records.

And mingling pleasantly was gorgeous Betty, the Donalds' slim, brown-eyed eighteen-year-old daughter. Her shoulder-length glossy coppery hair, full beautiful breasts, and bouncing walk almost denied who she seemed to be—and I was positive she was—a quiet caring sure person, older and wiser than her father and mother, older and wiser, I thought, than anyone else wherever she happened to be. In her, certainly, spirits nested. She worked as hard, but she was like a shadow beside her hearty, noisy parents. They stomped, she glided. You could talk and she'd listen and respond attentively, but not talking was just as welcome. Betty liked other people all right, but her self seemed really to be enough: in two months I never saw her irritated, angry, sad, bored, or flustered, only cheerful and calm. I have to say, though, that at times she did look dreamy, absent—as if she were waiting. After supper she might wander off along the lake's shore, stopping and bending to look at things, to touch them, growing smaller in the twilight. Young men asked her out often. A few times I'd accidentally seen her then in her slip or panties-and-bra rushing to dress, and I had turned away, which I didn't when she lay sleepily open to the sun on her back in a pale-blue swimsuit on the dock. When the spruced-up young men picked her up for dances and movies, I'd feel a bit sorry for them: they were so young.

One night she said I should come, too—to a dance in a barn. Dark and smoky and hot inside, it smelled of sweat and whisky; the music was loud, but mellow, clinging: no jitterbugging. Betty was greeted by many and flitted off amongst the dancers. Like the soldiers on the ship, young men stole longish swallows from Orange Crush bottles filled with something that tasted—I was offered some—like sugary fire, delicious. Slouched Bogey-style against a wall, hands pocketed, I watched the crowded floor, watched what shoulders did. Footwork counted, I knew from Glen, but shoulder motion even more so. Then Betty was there saying, C'mon! I thought we did very well, shuffling around, not speaking, her soft blouse brushing my collarbone, my throat, her eyes calmly looking down, and her back feeling moist through thin cotton. When the music stopped I said, Excuse me, and hurried out. It was awfully hot in the barn and a little puking helped.

There definitely wasn't one special young man: I would've known. Some nights when Betty was out I waited up for her in my room in the dark—if I left my light on, she'd knock after she got in and her hand would come around the door with a "nightcap" of milk or Coke. I'd hear the car coming, scoot out of my room, down the porch stairs, and, mosquitoes swarming, hide behind a tree. I had no qualms about this because I was in

love with Betty and had pretty well decided to marry her as soon
as I was old and wise enough. It wasn't feverish as with Jean, but
calm and sure like Betty herself and, of course, no one knew
about it. So really, I was only spying on my wife-to-be and that
was okay. They were wretched moments, though, waiting to see
if she'd let some son of a bitch kiss her good night, but I never
saw it happen. The swine might reach for her but she had a
quick way of raising her hand to his face, touching it, saying
something, and then turning and with long steps making for
the house. They could've necked along the way, of course—I'd
heard about necking by then, about what it could lead to,
about putting your hand on them or, God, right there—but
that thought, that picture, of a scrunched-up Betty in a car
kissing and so on, had to be squelched, could not linger.
Anyhow, it didn't suit her: she was too old and wise. And also, I
was sure, she'd want space around her, necking. The nights of
summer passed and I contentedly loved in silence. By all means,
let her have fun, go out with older guys. I'd wait. Wasn't she
waiting, too? What I did do every night was leave my door ajar—
just in case she ever had a sudden wild urge to slip in noiselessly
and kiss *me* good night. A nice fancy to drift off with.

Mid-summer and Mr. Donald, always thinking, came up
with a big new assignment: paint the "goddamn rowboats."
There were nine and by the time I left the lodge I'd painted
them all a handsome blackish green, inside and out. I worked
alone, not sharing the chore with anyone. I'd drag a boat ashore
and paint it in free time between other tasks; I got up earlier
and painted before breakfast, painted after supper until the sun
went down. Painting, I stripped to swimming trunks and tanned
deep brown. Every brush stroke refreshed old wood and I
advanced measurably. Mr. Donald was pleased. There wasn't

anything I could compare painting rowboats to. It wasn't play. It wasn't work. What could be finer than painting rowboats in the sun? Once the dipping and brushing had a rhythm, there was nothing that could still so completely. Even a fifteen-minute session slowed down time to what seemed hours. Sun burning, wind cooling, lake lapping, birds singing, thoughts roaming. I was asleep but very awake, and drained of all want. Often I wasn't even there at Rice Lake. Thoughts flowed lazily back and forth, far back and to the immediate now, fading or flashing crystal clear. There were moments when I felt I understood everything.

SIX / Separate Paths

MY MOTHER WAS A GREAT SECRET-KEEPER. To tell her something private was like telling a grave. Because "Anna can be trusted" women in camp had unburdened themselves to her, as had the brides in London. She was also close-mouthed about some things in her own life; a few she might reveal much later—like Grampa forgetting to send enough money to England for train fare—but the rest she kept to herself. They were, I thought, mostly what she called "not-nice things"; she disliked hearing those or telling them. She had probably said If-you-don't-have-something-good-to-say-don't-say-anything fifty-thousand times to Jerry and me. And so, when I got back to Osborne Avenue from the lodge I heard the wonderful news unspoiled: she'd found us, can you imagine! a house of our *own* to live in! Our own *address*!

She didn't let on, not to Jerry either, the "secret" behind it. When I eventually did find out, it sounded an icy note, but, by then, it didn't matter any more. What I learned was that, when we'd been in Canada only about two months, Grampa had called my mother into the parlour for a chat. Gramma had asked him to talk to her, he said, because it was just too hard for her. Gramma had said this to him: If only the boys had arrived sick and thin and Anna had an arm missing or an eye, it would have been so much easier to cope. But the boys were healthy

137

and rambunctious and Anna so strong and peppy! It's too much for your mother, Anna, Grampa had said. Sometime soon, you and the boys will have to move.

She hadn't written me the news on purpose, my mother told me now, to keep it a surprise. Our new house wasn't big. It was very small, but we would be boss there and independent. We were going to move right away. It was sad, of course, to leave Grampa and Gramma, and they thought so, too; they'd miss us, they'd said, but we'd visit often. There were fields all around the house and Lake Ontario just down the hill—a sled hill! We'd have our own shower and toilet! Damn, we'd be happy! She was going to be a supply teacher (no money yet from Daddy), Jerry could stay on at Malvern, and I, well, I'd get to go to a new school! Her excitement was catching. Time at once picked up speed, and it pressed out of mind Rice Lake's special quiet; days began to trot and then to gallop. I thought I'd probably miss Ronnie and Miss Tock, but the kids in the new school, as long as I didn't talk too much, didn't try to play football or hockey, would never know I wasn't an ordinary Canadian boy now.

Our landlord's corner house was on the south side of Kingston Road, bus stop 16, across from a thick patch of maple trees in a gully flanking the red-brick building of the Scarborough Foreign Mission Society. Like Mr. Donald, the landlord had put up huts on his property, just four, but from the outside his looked like little log cabins. My mother happened to come by in early summer and her intuition had cried Stop the bus!—she'd been hunting for extremely cheap quarters for weeks. Kingston Road was a busy highway really, the landlord, a plumber, told her, and he rented his cabins nightly to tired motorists; it was a new try-out summer-business called a Motel. So the cabins were empty in winter? she'd asked. Yes, come fall he'd lock them up. She'd like to rent one then, she said. No way, she'd freeze to death—they were built to be *cool* in *summer.* If he put in a little stove, she asked nicely, he'd be making money in the off-season, yes? And so they made a deal. She was probably wearing her hat.

We lived there that autumn and for half the winter in a space as big as one of Grampa's front bedrooms: two rooms separated by a narrow cubbyhole holding the toilet, shower stall, and toy-sized sink. A tiny Quebec coal stove heated our mother's room which was also the living room. Meals she cooked on a two-burner hot plate; we built a clothes-dryer of sticks and wire to fit around the stove. It was *gezellig* and all we missed was a radio: a radio would've been the finishing touch. People said it was a rough winter and several times the landlord had to shovel us free; the toilet bowl's surface froze in the night as did, in Jerry's and my room, the day's socks, underwear, and shirt armpits. This was how the pioneers had lived, but a lot worse, our mother told us, and wasn't it a "damn adventure?" And it was, and we *were* independent, and she'd kept another promise. And always ahead every few weeks was a Holway Sunday supper, an hour-long, bus-streetcar-bus trip now, and a little less often a short Saturday-afternoon cup of tea at Grampa's and Gramma's.

Ronnie visited one fall day and we roamed along Scarborough's spectacular bluffs, like a great fort's forbidding walls guarding Lake Ontario. Freighters plied the flat steely water but never a sail. Ronnie had grown taller with heftier forearms over the summer, but he still seemed a boy who had no bad thoughts. School, part-time jobs, sports, movies, and so on were fine subjects, but they weren't what my head was bursting with. By then, though, I couldn't talk about it with

Ronnie, nor with Jerry, not even Glen. Too late: it was so private it was secret. To be honest, sometimes those days I thought I was a little, or maybe a lot, besotted.

The new school didn't help much. At Midland Avenue Public School I might not have differed in accent and clothes any more, but there was really no way I could hide the gaps in everyday street and school background. I hadn't, I had to admit, managed to become an entirely ordinary Canadian boy after all: kids caught a whiff of "foreignness." The ones who noticed least and cared least were usually the dumbest and also often the toughest—and I drifted to them, in the yard and after school. The guys weren't camp-tough certainly, but, as un-Ronnie as could be, they smoked, swore, spat, fought, pissed in the schoolyard when no one was looking, played hooky, wrestled girls to the ground, drank beer at night (they said), jeered teachers, messed up the school, and stole comics, pin-up magazines, and cigarettes from variety stores. Talk was mostly about girls—not the actual girls, just a few of their parts and what those were good for—on and on about their tits, cunts, asses, and "whacking off," "feeling up," "getting laid." Though mentioned by name, the whole girls, those right there in the yard with faces and laughs, weren't really discussed, not even Big Rose with her carrot-coloured hair. Soldiers' talk on the ship used to get rough and Glen could make himself clear, but this was talking dirty: not uninteresting at first, but after a while it seemed just lifeless fancy.

Jane Russell didn't help either. Pictures and posters appeared of her that fall advertising *The Outlaw*, a Western. Hair wild, mouth pouting, and looking hard-as-nails lovely, she leaned back into hay, full breasts straining inside a shoulderless "outlaw blouse," thighs hidden in the fake black shadow of a hiked skirt. I never saw the movie, but in our freezing bedroom I lay awake seeing Jane as the perfect guide on a dangerous dark path I could follow, if I chose, with Betty (or Rita Hayworth) beckoning on the safe and lighted one. Jane's path hadn't been explored, Betty's a little bit. I'd arrived at a fork in the road, I felt, and had to choose. Or could you walk both paths at once? No, I was sure they curved away from each other. Could you trundle along one for a while, and then switch? Could you just go back and forth as the mood hit you? Or was this a stick-to-it choice? When Jerry's reading lamp was still on I could see my breath. Now he was asleep. Did Jerry know about paths? I wasn't sure. Paths would be very hard to explain, to Jerry, to anybody. Why be so hot and bothered about paths at all? Still, if it really had to be an absolutely forever decision, there was no choice . . . but then Jane's path would always stay a mystery, the false shadow would never yield, and what all else, unheard, unseen, unsmelled, untouched, untasted, would I be missing? Jesus! Could *that* be right? It needed sorting out, but *could* it be sorted out? In my head the sultry Jane murmured Fusspot! and winked.

There was no reason to call her Big Rose; she wasn't tall or wide, just chunky. She was a grade above me in Eight, lived somewhere down our sleigh hill, and she was tough, no question. When guys chased and pushed her in the yard—and at recess they were around her like flies—she'd yelp and ram them right back. If they grabbed her she'd actually wrestle the odd one to the ground first and, panting and grinning, pin him down, knees grinding into the muscly part of his upper arms; but even if, as usually happened, it was her on her back squirming to get away, she'd still be grinning. She was strong and she liked wrestling and she liked boys. Small orange curls fell around a full-cheeked small-nosed face so freckled it was almost brown, and she wore red or brown trousers, bright-coloured hunting jackets, and bulky red sweaters like the card-playing Polish mom on the ship. She smoked, she swore, and if anyone went too far she'd scream like a cat. She screamed often. In the wrestling, hands groped at her chest, at her crotch; it was a good thing she didn't wear skirts: as it was, Big Rose's parts were remarked on more than any other girl's. Guys said the screams were for show though, that if you got her alone she probably didn't scream, that she'd be quiet as a mouse. I believed the first bit, but how would they know about the second? They didn't. "Probably" gave them away. They were guessing.

Canada's winter, spring, and summer had been fine, and then came the grand surprise of the blazing trees of fall. It had already snowed once, but under a cloudless sky the maple stand by the Foreign Mission Society was still in full autumn glow. On this day, I was squatting on cold wet ground behind bushes there. Trotting the mile and a half home from school, I'd washed my face, brushed my teeth, and come down to wait, heart hammering. My mother and Jerry wouldn't be in from the city for another hour. I thought she might slip through the trees to get to where she lived down the hill: kids take short cuts. In my mind buzzed an alarm set at low, Wwwwrrrronnnggg! I shook my head to shut it off. *What* was wrong? What *could* be wrong? Nothing was wrong. I was a curious boy, that's all. A curious *insane* boy. The buzzing started again, but too late.

Her clothes and hair blended with the yellows and reds and the orange of the maples. Head down, Big Rose trudged along, schoolbag in one hand, cigarette cupped in the other. Taking a deep breath, I jumped out in front of her.

Shit! she yelped.

Hi! I said, smiling as wide as I could.

She'd stopped dead, shoulders and arms bent, hands open, very ready. Small blue eyes stabbed into the trees and behind her, checking for other crazies.

Bugger you! she snarled. What's going *on*?

Nothing, Rose. Honest!

I'd never spoken to her before. Leaves twirled down. Kingston Road traffic moaned. In the crisp air I was sweating. Also trembling a little. Was I being really stupid? She took a couple of steps towards me, and let the schoolbag drop.

What nothing, Ernie! I'd scared the shit out of her!

That wasn't true. She wasn't scared. A bit angry maybe, but not scared. And she knew my name.

I was sorry, I said. I saw her coming and was just saying Hi.

She took a hard puff from her cigarette, eyes darting, then stopping on my face. Her freckles ran right into her hair.

No, I was lying, she said, but in a less tight voice. I'd been waiting for her, she said, waiting right there in the goddamn bushes. Waiting for what, Ernie?

No, honest, I wasn't waiting—and *sorry*, I said again, and reached out to give her shoulder a "sorry" pat, but she moved in closer and shoved my hand away. We were standing inches apart, and she was breathing fast. God! was she going to beat me up in a minute? The trees were so dense no one could see through them.

Waiting for *what*, Ernie?

Just to say Hi, honest.

Jesus, I was lying again. Liar! *Just to say Hi, honest*, she mimicked, but she was grinning a little. She hated liars, I should know.

Just being friendly? I tried.

Yeah, sure.

Just being nice?

The trembling was fading, but not the heart-thumping.

Nice, huh?

She let the cigarette butt fall, ground it out with her boot.

Just having fun?

Fun, huh?

That's all.

It's hot, she muttered, and zipped down her hunter's jacket.

Did she always come by this way, through the trees? I asked just to say something.

Okay then, she said with a sigh, what did I want?

She and I seemed suddenly very alone together. The sound of the traffic had died.

Not a thing, Rose.

Don't lie, Ernie.

Nothing. Honest!

Okay then, she said with another sigh, but this first, okay? There was no warning. In one fast move she hoisted her red sweater and stretched-taut white bra to her chin, and full, freckled, and brown-tipped they tumbled free bobbing.

"Kiss 'em," she murmured.

And I did at once, leaning forward on tiptoe, hands at my sides, eyes shut, softly, very softly, because they might break, one, and then the other, just brushing them, one, and then the other, only feeling their heat, one breast, and then the other breast, on and on, not stopping, not even when I felt small wrenches from her body, a leg lifting, and then, as we sagged to the ground, a sharp tugging at my belt, at my pants—no, I only quit when her nakedness below moved a little, a little, against mine, because I then sort of fainted. Well, not fainted, I just went away for a moment, a soundless marvellous dive in the dark. I opened my eyes a minute or an hour later and where was I?—but the world really hadn't changed at all since I'd closed them. We lay on moist leaves, heads close, Rose on her back staring up, breasts lifting, a complete stranger.

"You okay?" she asked, speaking to the treetops.

She rolled away, sat up, and set to straightening and pulling her clothes down and up, brushing herself off, and so did I. We had our backs to each other. What now? Was I supposed to say something? *Thank* her? Ask, Can I see you again? But I didn't want to see Rose again. Not after what just happened. Sure, I'd say Hi at school, but not *see* her, no, or probably talk to her much. Because, Jesus! what had just happened? I was shocked, to be honest, a bit disgusted; also with myself, sure. But what nice girl would just tell you to kiss them . . . and then, for God's sake, I heard her *humming*! I swung around and watched Rose as humming she lit a cigarette, took a long drag, and scrambled to her feet, picked up her schoolbag, and began walking backwards away from me. Bye Ernie, she said, and turned and was swallowed by the blood-and-gold trees.

When my mother and brother got home, I had, like such an innocent kid, made tea and was practising my violin; later, I'd volunteer to do the dishes. I felt I had something to make up to them: I had a big secret and they had no idea. I'd looked at myself in the tiny bathroom mirror and thought, "I'm twelve and I've kind of done it," and felt a little proud and a little sick of myself, and a bit scared, too, remembering that *pull* to wait in the trees. A lonely thing, a secret. Mike the American probably had secrets. For the first time, I felt older than my brother and, also for the first time, knew I definitely couldn't confide in my mother, and so that evening, again for the first time, felt uncomfortable with both.

I took the violin into the unheated room to scrape on. That wretched violin—something else I could feel bad about. With still no money from Indonesia, she couldn't at all afford my lessons, the instrument's rent, the bus fare to classes. Her weekly earnings of about twenty dollars (*if* she was asked to teach every day) plus Jerry's and my after-school dollars (the summer's wages had gone for winter clothes) didn't stretch far. Yet, one offhand mention that I'd like to learn to play like Uncle Ralph, and she'd warbled, Great! You'll love it! Daddy'll love it! I'll find a teacher! Now I was sorry I'd opened my mouth. Like so much else that fall and winter, if it took some effort, it fairly soon got boring. I had no notion why, but so, by then, had classes in the new school grown tiresome. So had my ordinary-Canadian-boy routine. So had doing push-ups. So had the first book I set out to read, one of Glen's Zane Grey Westerns. So would, come winter, trying to skate on Glen's old skates, trying to ski on Glen's old skis, sledding. Only girl-thoughts I didn't let go of— oh, and comics and movies and smoking. Knowing nothing of what I thought I should know, I'd burned to know *everything* for more than a year, afire almost in summer on Rice Lake where time slowed down. Now time felt like it was racing, and, well, maybe I was just fizzling out. More and more not-knowing and always-being-behind felt like that's-how-it-has-to-be. A swiped piece of life wasn't recoverable after all; I'd never catch up, so why bother? I thought dead Hubie probably would've agreed. And so I quit the violin in January having learned a few bars of "Silent Night, Holy Night" I'd already known how to play years ago on a harmonica I used to own.

Loafing and dawdling was what I was doing—even knowing it got worse the longer I kept it up, and harder to snap out of. On New Year's Eve, wanting to stop, I wrote up a list of curt resolutions for 1947: exercise, study the violin, be better-mannered, don't talk so much, be good to Mom, do things alone, stop eating junk, write Dad every week, don't run away. But, except for the last, they went unheeded. It vaguely occurred to me to run away when I felt uneasy with my mother and brother, usually after I'd done or thought bad stuff. They were both incapable of that, I was sure, though Jerry did have girl-thoughts, we'd shared some, but his were so mild compared to the ones I kept to myself; maybe not even Glen's could match those. But run away to where? Cowboy country? Each time I lazily played with the idea, it fell apart. So . . . let's say I'd hitch-hiked on trucks into the hills of Alberta. So I arrive at the ranch—early misty morning, chimney smoking, sausages frying, a slim ranch wife, a shy daughter in a soft-leather shirt. Sit you down! says the wife. Coffee? Joe'll be right in. Cream? No, thank you, ma'am, I take it black. Then rancher Joe stomps in, a tall lean dusty narrow-eyed man of few words, hard but fair. For a long time he says nothing, eats his eggs and sausages. Wanna be a cowpoke, huh? he finally drawls. Well, son, I gotta ask—boots, neckerchief, long johns, hat, lasso, chaps, gun, spurs, saddle, you got 'em? Can you ride, son? Can you rope, brand, fix a fence, roll your own, shoot a rattler, *make* black coffee? I can roll my own, sir. Go home, son. Get off my land!

Loafing and dawdling in Kingston Road stores; drinking pop, eating candy, twice slipping comics under my jacket and slouching out. I stole a comb, too. What *for*? I had a brushcut. My mother made me take it back. Guys said you could quit school at sixteen, go to work (factories paid well), rent a room, have girls over, buy a car. It sounded sensible, but was four years away. So, always looking attentive, I mostly didn't hear, see, or speak in class. I did try to talk to Rose and then gave up: she was polite but cool, as if I was a stranger. In January she stopped coming to school. I saw her once, on the sledding hill, looking heavier, grinning and sliding on its frozen surface her arms around a guy in his twenties also wearing a hunter's jacket. The days flowed by one much like the next; and evenings, too, shut in the cabin, Jerry at his homework, he and my mother tired from their daily treks into Toronto. Less and less stirred for me. And in this sluggish time, my father wrote sternly from Batavia that *his* father in Holland, Grootvader, had scolded *him* by letter for the atrocious Dutch in *my* letters. As long ago as spring, our mother had begun pressing Jerry and me to write the other grandparents—Grootvader and Tante Cox, our divorced Dutch grandfather and his second wife, and Grootmoesje, his first wife, my father's mother. Yes, we didn't know them, but it was family duty and, she insisted, they loved us. So every two months we scribbled reports on our health, on school; the replies, it has to be said, were equally drab. Keep up your Dutch! my father urged from oceans away. Read Dutch! Write Dutch! Oh sure, I was going to worry about Dutch when now even the relish for English was dimming. Bugger Grootvader! My father also noted that drawings in my letters to him took up a lot of writing space. Was I lazy or did I have so little to tell him? Well, yes—so no more drawings and larger writing.

In mid-March our mother asked, Shall we move? She and Jerry were spending just too much time (and money) travelling, and lack of private space in the half-frozen cabin was making all three of us twitchy. Yes, we said. To the Beach then, friendly

Holway turf, so Jerry could stay on at Malvern, to a run-down house on Fernwood Park Avenue, a quiet short street near the lake, and into two small sunny second-floor rooms plus kitchen with our own stove and fridge. Balmy Beach Public School was five minutes away and the cheerful Chinese family's grocery store where I at once found work even closer. A father, mother, and three teenage daughters, I'd never seen people work so hard, except prisoners. Tallying my first evening's delivery payments at the cash register, I came out a cent ahead, shrugged, and dropped it in the penny slot. "No, no, no!" laughed the father, pressing the coin back into my hand. "Ten of these, Ernest, make a dime!"

Balmy Beach smelled as nice as Kimberley and Midland and in class I acted as alert as I had in both. But starting the first week, I was absent often because of sudden headaches, stomach-aches, sore throats, blackouts, and so on. Playing hooky meant lying to teachers and to my mother, which was new, but not so hard: always include a snippet of truth; never embroider. Sometimes notes were needed, but usually wide-open brown eyes did the trick. Once I took a razor-blade and scraped a spot on my forehead semi-raw—a "terrible fall" good for two days. With the flat to myself, I'd sleep late, read comics, drink tea, and, as chilled with the windows open for the smoke as in the cabin, listen for hours to a small old brown radio (borrowed from Aunty Ada).

In Grade Seven only Guy was sick as often as I was, surprising (and untrue, of course) because he was by far the biggest and strongest boy in school. At fifteen, grey-eyed and blond, Guy was a full-grown man; so was Glen, but Guy was a lot taller than Glen. Guy had the muscles and bulk to be a pro hockey player or heavyweight boxer, people said, said it to him, too, which was about the last thing he wanted to be or hear. What Guy liked was to be left alone and, because of his size, he usually was. Except, it seemed, by the aunt (no uncle) raising him who insisted he wear clean pressed clothes and polished shoes to school, shave every day, and, above all, attend. In class Guy sat stiffly upright, staring, a half-asleep giant: it was all old news to him, as it had also been during his second year in Grade Six. He was just entirely uninterested in school, as I was, too, but at least I faked attention. Guy even ducked gym when he could, a relief to the rest of us—in action he was a quick smart *locomotive*! I watched him and listened in on some of his muttered absentee-excuses, but, while those were as lame as mine, teachers never questioned him, as if there was no point. I wondered what Guy did in his time off. During recess he usually wandered away alone for a smoke. One day I followed and, as one "player" to another, nervily asked what he did with his hooky time. He looked down at me, eyes a bit vague, face closed, a strong face of squares, square chin, square nose, square cheeks. I thought he'd tell me to bugger off, but no, he muttered (he always muttered) that he didn't do much. He couldn't stay home because his aunt was there, so he took walks or, if it was cold, had coffees in restaurants. Now, with spring coming, he'd go down to the beach. That was *it*? I asked. Just about. Well, my speed exactly, I thought—and in the remaining months of school, he and I now and then took off do-nothing afternoons and even whole days at the same time.

We'd buy pop on Queen Street and carry it down to the boardwalk. If we passed girls, their eyes, just as with Glen, slid to Guy only. I didn't mind. Though smaller and dumber, at thirteen, I'd begun to hang around with older guys, felt more at ease with them. Guy and I would hunker down in quiet spots because I stood out during school hours; not him, of course. As in class, he'd sit straight and still, on a rock, a bench, and, when it got warmer, on the sand or grass, trousers neatly lifted, polished shoes aligned like a military man's. In his heart, I thought, Guy really wanted to be a sloucher, but that marvellous body wouldn't let him, nor, probably, his aunt. He wasn't much of a talker, or much of anything that I could make out, but he seemed content then. We'd sit with our backs to the city, forget the city after a while, and watch the grey water, the sky, and, from the corners of our eyes, boardwalk strollers, and say not a word for the longest time. Restful that. Occasionally, if not pushed, Guy might answer a question, always briefly; he never asked any: he wasn't curious. I wasn't sure why I played so much hooky, so I asked once why he did.

He couldn't stand being made to learn, he said, and that's what school did. He couldn't stand being *made* to do anything.

I thought that made sense. I'd felt like that. And it proved me right that Guy wasn't a bad student because he was stupid or slow or lazy. He just didn't care for discipline. My father'd love him!

But what about his aunt? Didn't she . . . ?

Never mind his aunt.

Guy almost never mentioned her—I didn't know her name—or anything, really, about his home life or younger days. He steered clear of himself. So, sometime later, I led up to another question, carefully.

Did he have a girlfriend?

Nah.

Ever had one?

Nah. He couldn't get serious about "the ladies." Too young. He *liked* them though?

Oh sure.

That I was pleased to hear: it had worried me. With Guy's looks and build, every girl in school would've gone out with him. Ignoring other guys and teachers was one thing, but he shunned girls, too. Had I understood what he said? The girls at school were just too young, and so was he, to go out, or, they were too young, or he was too young, to get serious, or what? But the topic was done with.

Days were stretching, and Jerry and I started thinking about summer jobs. He found one quickly as an office boy at Canada Dry Ginger Ale. I was going to write to Rice Lake, but then came word via Aunty Ada's dairy that two brothers could use me on their farm north of Toronto. No Betty, yes, but better pay, Sundays off, and it meshed perfectly with Glen's staying-in-shape and independence truths. Take it, Glen urged. By summer's end I'd be an Experienced Farmer! What more could a man want?

I asked Guy what he thought.

Farming was okay. He'd farmed himself.

Was he looking for a job?

Yeah.

What kind?

Factory, but year-round.

Year-round?

Well, he'd be sixteen soon. . . .

Jesus! What about his aunt?

Never mind his aunt.

It wasn't such a surprise. I didn't like school much, but Guy really hated it.

He'd get his own place?

Sure.

A car?

Sure.

I thought it sounded fine. On your own, free. A car or, better still, a motorcycle. I could actually be Guy in four years. But something nagged.

What if the factory boss *made* him do stuff?

Nah, a boss just wanted you to do the job right.

But what if the boss *made* him, say, learn to work a new machine?

Well, too much bossing, and he'd take off.

I thought of the Chinese grocer, of Mr. Donald. Bosses who bossed. Do this, do that! When you looked around, bosses were everywhere. At school, work, home. My father was a boss, my mother could be, Guy's aunt was one—and *they* had bosses, too. Everybody had a boss. Guy was going to have a hell of a time in his factory and, after he quit, in the next factory, and in the next.

So he had his own place, a car, and then what?

Nothing. You lived.

Meet a girl?

Sure.

Get married?

Sure.

Kids?

Sure.

Kids cost though, so how would he . . . ?

Never mind kids.

Too many questions. Anyhow, there was a sea of time before I had to make the Guy decision. No need to worry. A motorcycle, though, would be terrific.

The last time Guy and I played hooky together was a hot, drizzly Friday afternoon two weeks before the end of school.

He'd cut most of the morning as well and when I met him, about two at the end of Queen Street where the streetcar turned around, he was another Guy. Sweating, pale, hair mussed, shirt out of his pants, smelling gamy, drunk as a skunk.

He was celebrating, he announced and slapped my back, a bit hard.

Celebrating what?

He scared me a little, he was so different.

Everything! His aunt, for once, was out of town. Freedom in two weeks. A downtown job. Great pay. It was all *starting*!

Without checking traffic, he trotted across the street and into waist-high soggy grass behind a shed by the turn-around track. I followed. From his back pocket he dug a small bottle, unscrewed the top, and held it out.

Rum. Have a snort. There was more. And beer.

I tasted it. Fire strong and sweet.

Guy grabbed the bottle, took a gulp, another gulp, and threw it in the grass.

C'mon! Couldn't keep the ladies waiting!

And they were waiting, just a few doors away on the south side of Queen, in a dark basement room smelling wetly of smoke and perfume. Two of them, uncombed and barefoot in loose cotton shifts lolling unsmiling on a chesterfield bed; at least twenty years old, they had white legs and faces filmy from the heat. Somewhere in a corner a radio played softly. Besides the bed, there was a low round table loaded with glasses and bottles and ashtrays, some pillows scattered on a black rug, and a rocking chair draped with women's clothes. Two shaded lamps on the floor and a tiny window near the ceiling gave light. Guy flopped on the bed between them, and took away a tinkling glass from one. I sat down crosslegged on a pillow.

Party time! Guy shouted and drained the glass. Then he lurched up again and, sitting on the bed's edge, kicked off his shiny shoes. No socks.

Was I the friend? asked the woman without a drink in a slow voice.

I was a kid, mumbled the other, her eyes closed.

I was an okay kid, Guy told them.

Acting up, he moved on hands and knees to the table. There he sloshed hard stuff into glasses, chucked in ice-cubes from a bucket, dribbled Coke. He handed the drinks around with deep bows, then sagged back down on the bed. There was a tiredness in the room.

Party time! Guy said in his mutter.

He leaned across the chest of the slow-voiced woman, put his glass on the floor, and started lazily necking with her. The one with her eyes shut, curled away from them, tucking her hands between her knees.

I sat on the pillow and sipped from my glass. I'd turned my back but could hear little moans and sighs. So this was the life, eh? Dust on the high-up little window blurred the daylight, moonlight wouldn't have a chance. It was like being underwater in the room; hell no, it was like being in a jail! I swilled down my drink, placed the glass on the table without touching the others, and noiselessly escaped.

Blind at first in the bright outside, I swayed home fast, puked a little, and crept into bed—where I'd told the teacher I'd be anyhow, with my "splitting headache," which it really was by the time my mother and brother got in.

A bad evening, as it turned out, to feel poorly as well as to have trouble meeting their eyes. I knew I'd done nothing wrong in the basement—except drink the rum—but still, something had been off down there and, even if not for long, I'd sat and calmly breathed it in. So, when my mother broke the big news during supper, she and Jerry chatted on, and I sat rubbing my temples. What was there to say, anyway? In a flash we were back where we'd started: waiting for promises to come true. Had we ever left? "Normal living" on Obsorne Avenue, *sure*, then in the freezing cabin, *you bet*, then here on Fernwood Park Avenue, *hah!* We had *never* made it. Promises—shit! A letter from Batavia, boys: *great* news, boys! Daddy wanted us to come back to Indonesia. Just as he and she had always promised, we'd be a complete family again. Imagine! The four of us! Together! Daddy had rented a house, was filling it with furniture. Getting passage money over wouldn't be easy, but he worked for the goverment, and it had promised to help. Going home, boys, *home!* Sure we were—for the umpteenth time. I wasn't so thrilled to be returning to my father either. He had faded because of time and distance but also because his letters connected less and less. They always noted how hard he worked, how tired he was, how his life was so difficult all alone; I could *hear* the sighs. Yet, I knew he loved his work, had sailed Dutch lakes all the days of a three-month government-paid furlough, and, back on Java, spent many weekends in the cool mountains always, it seemed, to prevent in the nick of time, in his words, "total collapse from exhaustion." Well, his life didn't sound that terrible to me. So, along with the talking-tos in his letters, I'd come to resent the whimpers, and the letters were about all that was real of him, for me.

It was true, though, that we'd always known we'd return one day—but, I thought, when had any of us last mentioned it? And just then my mother reminded me of something. We were still at the kitchen table, she and Jerry talking. She was saying our summer jobs were safe because we wouldn't likely be sailing until fall, but we shouldn't plan on going back to school; fine with me, though Jerry looked a bit sad: he liked Malvern. But then she said, just chattering, that even if departure was very sudden, you know, we wouldn't, thank God, have much to pack; we'd be ready in a jiffy. But I remembered a few times, in the cabin and on Fernwood Park, when offhand she'd said that she was going to save up to buy, say, a new frying pan, a lamp, or a dish rack; she hadn't in the end, but had definitely meant to. Now why, if you're poor, I asked inside my throbbing head, even think of buying such things, things you could do without, things you wouldn't want to lug around, if it was certain that sometime in the fairly near future you were taking off across the world? But that question was smothered in a rush of anxious others. What goddamn use would ordinary Canadian boyness be in Indonesia? Or almost accentless English? Or Glen's truths? Or a grasp of baseball? Or delivery-boy tactics? Or knowing how to pamper strangers secretly or paint rowboats? And, at the end of summer, what bloody use was an Experienced Farmer? Jesus, I didn't want to leave!

And it was just as well then that, a few weeks later, the Armstrong brothers, starting day one, hour one, worked me so hard on their farm that Indonesia was sometimes wiped clear away for days on end. Also, as Jerry and my mother seemed glad to be going and I wasn't, it was maybe just as well I wasn't in the city. The brothers let me change into old clothes and rubber boots on the morning of arrival, and then some beasts at once needed feeding and massive spills of their shit needed dumping on a fly-covered mountain behind the barn, nicely called "manure"; it was amazing how much of it horses, cows, and pigs could produce. A full shift, I found out next day, stretched from five a.m. to about seven in the evening (later, during harvest) with three half-hour meal breaks, and, I have to say, I didn't mind a bit, didn't once mind the whole two months the long hours and slogging labour. There was no ownership feeling as there had been on Rice Lake—the brothers would've been shocked: the place was *theirs*—but I quickly felt a useful part of it. This was because, first, every big and little job of work, once I got the hang of it, made such great good simple sense: I was helping grow food. And second, because Tom and Rick Armstrong worked unsparingly themselves and seemed, every day again, extremely contented men. Since they were untalkative, and not whistlers or hummers either, the way you could tell they were happy was by how, like patient, good-humoured parents, they handled animals, by how, as if they were friends, they wielded tools and operated machines, by how when they spied even the smallest thing amiss in the fields or the barn it was fixed instantly or very soon, as if it was a prized possession, by how they'd stand still and study the sky, for a minute, or two minutes, as if it was some fine painting, and, finally, by how they put away Tom's wife Mary's meals, as if they *deserved a mound* of porkchops on a platter, hours-old chilled milk, just-picked vegetables, sun-warm tomatoes, potatoes mashed with cream, and home-baked bread and pies, a choice of three, apple, blueberry, and, say, rhubarb.

Tall, blue-eyed men with hard hands, furrowed necks, and stubbly cheeks, they wore coveralls, black-and-grey-striped railway caps, and filthy boots left unlaced; when they rolled up their sleeves to wash, their arms showed bone white against browned hands. In his early forties, Rick was the oldest, blond-reddish, balding, a bit heavy; Tom was lean as a cowboy, had thick black hair, and, though a year or two younger, was the boss. Both did whatever needed to be done, but Tom made the decisions; or Tom and Mary did. Small, blonde, plump, and as quiet as her menfolk, Mary was one brother's wife, but, I thought, also a bit of a mother to both. Quick on her feet, she cooked, cleaned, washed, gardened, paid bills, and daily killed a thousand flies; there was a radio, but she seldom had it on. By eight, eight-thirty at night, Tom and Rick were upstairs "all tuckered out," as she called it, and me, too, in my shut-off room behind the kitchen, and the last sounds, mother sounds, were of Mary winding a clock, clicking lights, and padding up creaking stairs to join Tom.

In all my time I never heard an angry word amongst the three except once when a livid Mary, little chin trembling, called her husband and brother-in-law "stupid and childish and stupid!" That was late in my stay when we were harvesting corn and, with the combine rotating from farm to farm, neighbours and their hired hands had come to work our place. In the fields, between loads, we jabbed forks into the ground and found shadow to lie down in and smoke. They were all grown up men and some also chewed tobacco, which I hadn't seen before. One of the hands, a big young shirtless guy, chomped off a wad, then offered his tobacco to me.

Or was I too young?

No, I wasn't too young.

Did I know how?

Sure.

Birds twittered, crickets jumped, weathered faces listened deadpan.

You chew, and every ten minutes, you spit, right?

Sure.

I bit off a piece of the hard tobacco and set to chewing.

Every ten minutes, the hand reminded me helpfully.

In a moment my mouth filled with saliva and bitter juice, and I swallowed. Horses returned an empty wagon, and in the fierce sun we went back at it. After many swallows and just two spits, I had to lie down. Within the hour I was lifted onto a load of corn and run up to the house, sick for the rest of the day and most of the night. And Mary was furious. From my bed I heard her ranting to herself, and then at Tom and Rick during supper. Men were so stupid and childish and stupid!

It was mostly Tom who showed me my chores in the early days, usually only the once and with few or no words. That unnerved me at first, but it was just his way; Rick's way, too, when he had to demonstrate something. Since they were little kids the two had worked the farm—full-time as teenagers after their dad died—and for them nearly every task had grown into an old habit as simple as brushing teeth—what was there to say? And I didn't mind that, either: everything on the farm finally had logical purpose not so difficult to track down. Glen was right, about staying in shape, about independence: a farmer's life was a hell of a life.

Very quiet men, the brothers, but friendly, and funny. They never let up on work so there was no "horsing around" as on Rice Lake; instead, wordlessly, they often teased each other, like boys, and me, too, after a while. It was mostly pranks, a small stock of harmless, maybe mindless pranks they'd played over and over on one another through the years with, it seemed, only two rules: no frightening animals and no instant revenge—that would slow the work-flow. One brother might be sitting half under a cow milking, when the other came along carrying a pail of water somewhere, stopped, splashed, oh, a glassful down the milker's neck, and walked on. Or, at the kitchen door a brother kicked off his boots before going in for lunch and, half a minute behind him, the second brother tossed the boots around the side of the house or under a tree—easy to spot but needing to be fetched in socks. Barn lights were suddenly doused, barn doors unexpectedly locked, a tool's handle oiled, hay pitched on a person's head from the loft, the sugar pot hidden during a meal, the truck's engine made briefly unstartable, whatever. On and on. I laughed and cheered while the brothers, after so many years, managed at most to grin or snort or roll their eyes. After the war, prison-camp survivors said humour had been one of their best weapons. The brothers would've done fine there: they made time fly. As they always would, I guessed, until one day one or the other was a prankster left behind alone.

About half my Sundays off I didn't go home but helped (unpaid) with morning and evening chores and "churched" (Tom's word). In black suits and shaved, with Mary in a Sunday dress wearing lipstick, the family would, after the service, actually chitchat with neighbours, about crops, children, prices, weather, and always about a few dead people; farmers remembered for a long time people who had died. Back in Toronto each Sunday closer to autumn, there was no escaping travel talk, which I couldn't let on I didn't want to hear. In the after-dark bus returning, I'd chide myself, feeling a little sad, not to like the farm too much, not to let it get to me. People went away, things proved unkeepable, and it had to be like that, I argued, with places, too. And so, finally, when leaves turned colour and the farm didn't need me any more, it wasn't so hard to go. Mary hugged me in the house and tucked apples and pears in my jacket pockets. Tom and Rick walked me up to the highway to flag down the bus. We shook hands and they grinned and grunted something and Rick thumped my shoulder. I watched the brothers amble back down the road to their world. They didn't turn to wave: that would've been unlike them.

We started readying ourselves. Money had arrived. Tickets were waiting in New York City. There were goodbyes to say. I suppose in those last days we must have seen my mother's brother and his wife and children again. I looked up Ronnie; he'd become a very keen tennis player. Certainly there was a dinner with all the trimmings at the Holways. They saw us off at Union Station, too, as did Grampa and Gramma.

On a Saturday afternoon about two weeks before we left, Grampa and Gramma asked us to come visit, just Jerry and me. A duty visit, we thought, but no, we had a good time. In the parlour as always the curtains were tightly shut but, though it was a warm day, the fan wasn't turned on. Gramma served tea and cookies, and, as usual, there were longish moments when nothing was said, when Grampa pulled at his cigar and Gramma on her cigarette, when Gramma, as was her little habit, might repeat two or three times the last words she or Grampa had spoken.

You young fellows smoke, don't you? Grampa rumbled suddenly. Don't lie, he added, but not angrily.

Well, so what? I think went through both Jerry's head and mine. What's he going to do about it?

Gramma smiled at us.

We said yes, Grampa.

We knew it was goddamn bad for us, Grampa said puffing. We knew it was a dumb thing to do, but we bloody well smoked anyway, right?

We nodded.

Well, he and Gramma had decided that they didn't like us sneaking around. If we were going to smoke, then smoke right here. Have a cigar, he said, holding out the tin his came in.

That threw Jerry and me for a second, but we didn't let on.

Jerry said no thank you, but could he maybe have one of Gramma's DuMauriers? Grampa shrugged, sure.

Gramma offered her package smiling.

I chose one of the cigars, sniffed it. Grampa flicked his lighter, and I leaned over and lit up.

And so we sat there, the four of us, in the still hot air now turning blue. Conversation didn't flow all that much easier. Every few minutes Grampa asked if I was liking his cigar. I wasn't: it tasted sharp and hurt inhaling. It was a very good cigar, I said. But still we did for once, I believe, feel comfortable with one another that afternoon because, in a nice way, all four of us were amused. Grampa and Gramma thought they were putting something over on us, and Jerry and I knew what it was. The visit lasted for four or five cigarettes and two cigars. When we got outside I just managed to get out of sight of the house before losing lunch. Jerry, of course, was okay. We agreed it had been a good try on Grampa's and Gramma's part to get us to quit smoking, and also that it was very kind of them to have tried at all. It was, actually, about as fine a memory as could be to carry away with us.

SEVEN / A Way of Seeing

LONGING FOR CANADA wouldn't occur until the first time out alone on deck when, turning full-circle, there was nothing to see but the choppy Atlantic. An ache flared, then quietly settled in for the next several years. It wasn't a yearning for certain people or places but for something vague, for, having known it a while, the *promise* of Canada. What else to call it?

First, though, there were twenty-four hours in New York City to get through. Sitting up all night from Toronto, we arrived about eight—and Grand Central Station was unnerving. That mass of scurrying people was the most we'd seen in one place since the musters of shuffling internees in camp. In a vast roaring hall we froze like rocks for some minutes letting the busy Americans stream by. Where were we? How to get out? Near us another rock stood firm, a tall thin stooped man with hollow cheeks and eyes. My mother grabbed my arm. She knew him! She'd seen his picture! Jerry (who also read newspapers) said, That's the Dutch foreign minister, Mr. van Kleffens!

Go say hello! My mother pushed me forward. We're Dutch now!

I ducked into the rush and surfaced in front of him. He was studying a train schedule.

Goedemorgen, Meneer van Kleffens! Hoe gaat het met U? "Good morning, Mr. van Kleffens! How are you?" I said politely, smiling.

He looked up startled, then down at me, a small fellow Netherlander in the heart of the world's biggest city. The eyes were so sunken I couldn't tell their colour. He flapped the railway booklet at me.

Ga weg! Ga weg! "Go away! Go away!" he said hoarsely, and turned his back.

We waded out of the station and into New York. Our hotel was the Tudor (eighth floor) and the white-gloved old elevator man said the nearest best nightclub was The Glass Hat. On the train we'd agreed a nightclub was a must, a just-out movie on Broadway (plays were too dear) another, and, of course, the Empire State Building (the world's tallest structure). To find the last we wandered through great windy gorges of big and little Royal York Hotels; on the wide crowded sidewalks no one sauntered. Looking down a hundred-and-two stories, we saw narrow runs of ants and coloured cockroaches in the depths, but then a second later they disappeared—the Empire State Building *swayed*! My mother's cousin Gavin knew that already. He was waiting at the Tudor when we got back. The pleasant-enough fortyish bachelor son of Gramma's sister Florence, he'd come up from Philadelphia especially to visit. For hours of precious New York time he sat on one of the two beds talking family and drinking glasses of water.

The movie, *Unconquered* with Gary Cooper, started at nine so we'd get out only around eleven. Of course, said our mother, nightclubs always started late, as if this weren't a first for her, too. The taxi dropped us off about eleven-thirty at a small rakishly tipped neon high hat blinking in the late-autumn fog. Not a sound reached the sidewalk, but in the warm smoky air inside people shouted and laughed hard and saxophones crooned— *exactly* like in the movies! Our reserved table, small and round, edged the dance floor. Tired-bright eyes in pale faces watched the slender woman in the Oxford Street fedora and the teenage boys being seated. She ordered drinks, took out a cigarette, and the bigger kid couldn't dig matches out fast enough to light it for her; the other one sat scrunched up, hands in pockets. Eyes roaming, the three chattered non-stop. Kinda nice: a mom and her sons in a nightclub celebrating something.

The rye-and-ginger ale and two Cokes came in fluted glasses with coloured straws and orange slices wedged on the rim. A small dark woman with a boy's haircut sang songs about love that almost made her cry. Several times Jerry asked our mother onto the floor, and other dancers watched them, she happily out of sync, he straight-up, serious, a good-looking pair: they did fine. We left about one-thirty, striding arm-in-arm through mist to the Tudor Hotel.

The brand-new MS *Rondo* sported a yellow-banded black funnel and had just crossed from Holland to New York, but the New York–Batavia run was to be the Dutch freighter's first real working trip, her true maiden voyage. As the first passengers we'd live in gleaming luxury for forty days.

She could sleep twenty-three, but just thirteen passengers had booked, a mother with two daughters, six other younger women, a heavy-set middle-aged businessman, all Americans, and us. The mother and the six were joining husbands who worked in oil on Sumatra; the man was headed for Singapore; the daughters were Ann, thirteen, soft-voiced, slim, brown-haired, who moved in twirls and quick steps, and Joan, ten. At boarding in the early afternoon, the Chief Steward said the Captain and his officers would like to welcome us in the lounge at five, the cocktail hour. The girls' mother gave a little whoop.

By five it was dark, and the lights of New York harbour were receding behind us; always a bit sad, waning lights at sea. The lounge was in cream-coloured leather and dark red wood, the officers in trim black uniforms. We sat a little apart from the main group, and so did the businessman—alone at the bar where from then on he could always be found, dressed, it seemed, in a different suit and tie for every day at sea. The officers moved around, shaking hands, introducing themselves. They acted pleased that there were three Dutch-speakers along. My brother asked serious sensible questions of them. Jerry loved the sea, knew a lot about ships, and several of the men sat down for a few minutes. Soon, though, they circled back to the noisier tables of the American women. There was a party in the lounge that night. There'd be a party there nearly every night, even more often than on the *Devonshire*. As if anxious that, once on Sumatra, they'd never have fun again, the American wives couldn't party enough—the American man, too, by himself— and the one who partied hardest was the girls' mother, a large dark-eyed woman from Texas with glossy black hair always pinned up at the beginning of the evening. I sometimes watched, but the officers and women seldom danced; they played dice for drinks, sang, laughed, and as it got later couples wobbled away into the cabin corridors. The record the bar steward had to play more than any other, night after night, the song that resounded across the decks once portholes opened in warm waters, the song Jerry and I knew the ordinary sailors grew to hate, was "Give Me Five Minutes More."

Next morning three experiences began for my brother and me on the *Rondo*. Two we shared and they would fade, and one, different for each, would endure. I went up on deck after breakfast, while Jerry, of course, needed to check out the library in the lounge. I had my cheerless moment of longing, but it was cold and blustery so I came down to the lounge, too. Our mother sat in one corner reading, Jerry in another, the sisters in a third, playing cards. If it was rough the five of us would be the only ones there, but even in calm weather, few of the Americans straggled in before midday. Some of the women we wouldn't see until mid-afternoon; by then they'd have make-up on and be ready to party.

Jerry had his back to the room and a fat book in his lap. Amazing they had it here, he whispered; it was supposed to be tremendously dirty. He let me have a quick peek at the beautiful blonde on the cover in a low-cut old-fashioned dress and with pearls in her hair. No other passenger got a chance to read *Forever Amber* because we, I, kept it hidden in our cabin the whole trip. Jerry finished the long historical novel in a week. So-so, he said. Shut up in our bathroom (no light showing under the cabin door), I wrestled with it nightly, my first real book, but only dug up some burning looks, heaving bosoms, and violent embraces.

That first morning I also launched a romance with pretty Ann. In the lounge I asked her to go for a walk. We hid from the wind and chatted behind canvas-covered deck cargo, but quite soon she had to get back to her cabin; surprisingly, she said her mother was very strict. Could I see her again after lunch, after dinner? No, better tomorrow at the same time. And so we met once or twice a day, always in quiet hidden nooks. In the last two weeks on board, she sometimes let me hold her hand for minutes on end and to touch her cheek, once. What she did in those half-hours was flirt. Moist brown eyes dipping and sliding (like Amber's in the court of Charles II), she laughed, teased, and pouted, she skipped and swayed, her body trembly like a butterfly's. Even on hot decks in the tropics she never wore shorts, only modest flowery dresses; her long woman's fingers fluttered at the hems fending off the sea wind, denying glimpses of thigh. With her I felt older, more manly, but her whispery unreachableness often left me flustered and a bit tired. I accused her of it, too, of being a flirt.

Yes, Ernie, of course, she breathed.

Why?

Well, she had *Italian* blood.

Oh. Yes.

Starting on day one as well, Jerry locked into an incredible timetable when he stood a four-hour watch on the bridge. The evening before in the cocktail lounge he'd cornered the Chief Mate and begged permission and, until we docked in Batavia five weeks later, he worked an Apprentice Mate's full shift every day: four hours on, eight off. He was always tired and always happy. I'd never seen him so entirely content—like the Armstrong brothers on their farm. He smoked a tin of fifty cigarettes a day and drank black coffee with men. He let me visit sometimes and he *fitted,* a no-nonsense seaman plotting courses, working strange instruments, grumbling about the galley's sandwiches, shooting the sun, barking down a tube to the engine room, cursing when his relief overslept; in days, it seemed, he learned a whole new terse language about weather and navigation, as well as a slew of filthy jokes; bow-legged he paced the bridge, eyes set at long distance. They called him Hillen up there. So trusted did Hillen become that he was actually at the freighter's wheel on his last shift steaming into Tanjong Priok, Batavia's harbour, right up until the tardy pilot took over. He would always call this the journey of his life.

And, finally, on that same morning on the *Rondo* I had my first chat with Sparks. At the cocktail-lounge get-together, he had been one of the officers who briefly sat down with us. By far the tallest heaviest man there, with huge calm hands, he smelled of peppermint, and said he was the radio operator. He told us his name which I promptly forgot because he added his nickname, "Sparks." I liked that. The Dutch were stiff about names. Even adults usually used first names only with family or close friends. In camp, my friend Zuseke Crone, a mother of three, had one day invited me to call her Zuseke. It had been a present.

Jerry didn't have any of his good questions ready, so I threw one at Sparks.

What did he do?

He leaned across our table and suddenly his large blond balding head with the heavy-lidded blue eyes and the slight harelip was inches from my face.

"I talk to the world," he said softly, distinctly.

Whatever it meant—what an *answer*! I knew I was smiling widely.

He got up then, shook hands (the Dutch like shaking hands), and, bowing to the American women but not stopping, lumbered out of the lounge. He was seldom seen there again—never at parties—or, really, anywhere else on the ship. Like all the officers, though, when not on duty or asleep, he had to join passenger tables for dinner, on a rotating basis. In a few days, and spurred by the parties, that small group of people knew each other very well. But Sparks, saying little, politely smiled and nodded his way through meals, and didn't linger. The radio room, it seemed, was always calling. Which wasn't true. I'd find out that at sea or in port he was actually the freest man on board.

So, on that first day, when after some searching I found Sparks, he wasn't at the softly crackling radio desk, but in his open cabin next door, in an armchair, reading. Unsurprised, he shook my hand, waved me into the facing chair. Had he been waiting? I had the feeling he had, and would every time I visited—even, in weeks to come, when it might be the day's third or fourth pop-in. Small water-colour seascapes hung on the cabin's panelled walls and shelves were slatted so books stayed put in heavy seas.

Tea or water? he asked.

Water, please.

A brass-topped table by his chair was set with a teapot under a grass-green cozy, two mugs, a sugar pot, a carafe of water, and two glasses. He poured water, handed it across, and, smiling—why no moustache to cover that lip?—raised his tea mug in a salute. That little gesture, that first time, looked so familiar I had the sense I'd often seen him make it before. Nonsense, of course: he was a complete stranger.

Please, would I tell him my name again, Sparks said, swinging one long leg over the other. God, the *size* of those shoes! He asked where I was from and where I was going. Short-answer questions but, because of the intent way he listened, eyes rolling away, rolling back, he made me add whys, whos, and whats, and in minutes I'd outlined my whole damn life! I had listened like that to the soldiers on the *Devonshire*, except that, not understanding much, I'd faked it some. Watching Sparks listening, I felt sure he wasn't faking—and being really listened to was such a pleasure. How to listen well Sparks told me once later was easy: don't be in a hurry and tune out your own inner

voice. He often made a difficult thing sound simple and sometimes, afterwards, I wrote it down. That was because on an early
visit, Sparks had suddenly said that I should keep a diary—one
of two times he ever told me what to do. Unlike with most
adults, what he said wasn't meant to instruct, nor, I felt, did it
hold hidden lessons or veiled advice; he was just talking,
sharing what he knew, and, if something stuck, fine, my choice
entirely. Nah, I said, I'd already tried a diary as long ago as
London. Well, I was "riper" now, Sparks had insisted, and he'd
handed me a yellow radio-room notepad. A diary helped
memory, he said, and memory was *everything*. If we couldn't
remember our lives what did we have? I should write only for
myself, he pressed, but every day and never lie, that's all. And I
did, until the day we landed. I leafed through the diary once or
twice later in Batavia—mostly Ann stuff, but also entries such
as, "shut up inside to listen," "memory is all." I'd lose the pad, of
course, but some of Sparks's observations, even if only half-
understood, did sink in. With most I'd forget bit by bit whose
they really were; they became my own. But for a few I'd
remember the source. Remember, remember . . . he was so right.

I liked going on about myself, but that's not why I'd sought
Sparks out that morning.

How did he talk to the world?

One way is from there, he said, and went over to the con-
sole in the radio room. He twiddled a dial, flipped a switch, and
crazy blasts of chatter, squeals, and whistling came pulsing
through.

The world talking, Sparks said over his shoulder.

Turning the noise down, he murmured into a microphone
for a minute, then pulled a little machine forward on which,
with two fingers, he began tapping fast.

Talking to the world, he said.

And the other way? I asked.

With three long strides Sparks was back in the cabin.

On the air it was work, he said, but by living on ships he had a chance to talk to people from everywhere on every trip—for pleasure. He smiled.

I kept on with questions.

How long had he sailed?

Twenty-five years.

Where was his home?

Whatever ship he was on.

No, his *home*?

Yes, whatever ship he was on.

No home on land?

No, the closest was his brother's place, in Rotterdam.

Didn't it get lonely always on the sea?

Not lonely. He was alone a lot, but that he liked. There was so much to read, so much to think about. And remember, he found interesting people on ships, passengers, other seamen; always at least *one*. No, not lonely. If he could have his way, he'd be happy to sail the seas forever.

And women?

Women?

To marry one?

That could be a serious problem, Sparks admitted. He'd come very close a few times.

The first visit may have ended then, but I was back a few hours later. Every day, from then on, I whipped up to the officers' deck which held their cabins, the funnel, the radio room, and the bridge up front. Short calls usually, a glass-of-water or mug-of-tea long, whenever I had something to tell or ask, especially to tell. And always there was the sense of being expected. When it got warmer, we sat outside, shoving along our deckchairs inside the funnel's turning shadow. Brides, the plantation, Glen, floating, Michael, camp stories, the farm, snow, the swagger stick, Ronnie, scarred soldiers, Miss Tock, Hubie, whatever occurred to me, tumbled out, and there was Sparks, listening. And he, in turn, told of distant lands and of the half-dozen where we stopped. In every harbour, Sparks, looking down at brown-skinned dock-workers, said the same thing: Independence. They'll *all* want independence. By then, Pakistan and India had been free for several months; Indonesia was still trying.

Sparks had been to Indonesia often, before and after the war. Did he know about the spirits there?

Yes, he was familiar with them.

Was it possible that they sometimes left the islands?

They probably did wander off, yes.

I was pretty sure they hung around Rice Lake in Canada.

Why not? he said.

And then, of course, I had to report on the swearing Donalds, lovely Betty, painting rowboats in the sun—it was hard putting into words the marvellous feeling I had known then. Oh yes, oh yes, Sparks said, sitting upright, smiling, he recognized it! "Lucid serenity," he called it (in English). I was just lucky to have found it so young! And wasn't it always too brief? But once tasted, oh yes, you strove to taste it again, right? There was no greater delight, and, though difficult to find in ourselves, impossible to find anywhere else, right? He turned up his huge hands in question. What you thought, he said, wasn't that what you became? Wasn't it your own thoughts really that determined achievement, happiness, or suffering? And didn't you always have a choice? Good thoughts or bad thoughts?

Like most Dutch people, he was fluent in English, and our talk washed back and forth. He preferred English: Dutch could be so "raw." Of the two of us, I talked most by far. Sometimes, though, especially out on deck, we could also, as I had with Guy on the beach, sit and be quiet. There'd be the wind's low whistling and the slap of the sea and, stretched out in his white tropics, Sparks would look like a great whale. It was a true test, he remarked once, to sit in silence for a long time with a friend without growing tired of each other. Jews, he'd added, said that a friendless man was like a left hand without a right. Jews: the London film's skullmen had been Jews. No wise words from Sparks about that. Yes, he'd read a lot about Nazi horrors, had met survivors, too, but no, he didn't understand it. How to explain the boundless inhumanity of some, not so few, and those found everywhere? Could anyone explain it? All he did know, he said, was that he could never stop looking for an explanation; he felt it was a kind of obligation.

To be honest, sometimes Sparks lost me a little. But then, he could also free a shaft of light. Once I was telling him little Grampa-and-Gramma stories, the burnt chair, the smoke session, and then, not really meaning to—I'd never discussed it with anyone—I was describing the front-porch bawling-out. It had always puzzled me and, even as I was talking, I felt the story had no point, so I ended with a question.

Why was Grampa so angry with me?

The blue eyes veered away, paused, came back.

My grandfather had raised four children?

Yes.

Did I think he was a *bad* man?

Oh no!

Was my offence a big one?

No, little.

So why was my grandfather so angry?

The answer flashed out of nowhere.

He was angry at himself?

I said it as a question, as if I wasn't sure, but I was. It was true—although I couldn't for the life of me have said why.

Sparks nodded, nodded.

Was I right?

Yes, he said, he thought I was.

Later, alone, I wondered where the answer *had* come from, and why only *now*, and was it really *me* who said it? Yes, it was! Fucking amazing! I knew I'd discovered something deep—and by myself, too, so it was *mine*. Imagine, I could swirl people around in my mind, remember not-understood things said or done, and maybe fit the Grampa answer to them, too; I'd looked into adult mystery.

That little answer began to grow, and it wouldn't stop, because it started connecting with so much! It wasn't an answer, it was an explanation, and beyond that, it was a way of seeing. An adult man got angry with a boy because he was angry with himself. What else were adults angry with themselves capable of? Or even if just disappointed? Or, for that matter, if they were pleased with themselves? On and on. Fireworks in the brain! To think, a few weeks ago all I'd been able to manage was to concentrate in a dark bus on *not* liking the farm too much. And before that, the endless hours of sharing boredom with Guy. I'd been bloody asleep! I remembered the tag end of a sentence in a typed letter lying open on the dresser in our New York hotel room. It was my mother's letter, but I saw my name. My father had written, "I feel Ernest has too good an opinion of himself." Shit, how could he say that? He didn't *know* me! When he wrote it, I'd been about as sad and low as can be. Now Batavia was less than a week away. . . . But now also, I could ask myself, why had he written it? What was spooking *him*? Interesting, how the hurt of the words promptly faded. Half-joking, Sparks had told me at some point that he hoped he'd still live a long time because he was just starting to understand life a little. Me, too!

A full day, this. Jerry, Ann, and I had been up at dawn to watch the *Rondo* manoeuvring into a fishing village on the Sumatra coast. As jungle drew closer, the three of us were standing at a starboard railing, Ann in the middle. I was clasping her right hand with our arms straight down between us, so Jerry wouldn't see. She and her mother and sister were getting off, and it should've been a private goodbye moment. Why didn't Jerry get *lost*? But at one point he looked behind him for some reason and then, as his eyes swerved back, he saw. Jerry was seventeen, a man really, and he couldn't help smiling: he was holding Ann's *left* hand. He kindly waited until she'd disembarked to tell me and, at first, it wasn't funny—it hurt—but then, yes, it *was*, sort of. We compared notes. He'd also courted her from the first day; and no, she'd never let him kiss her either. We agreed that Ann, only as old as I, had daily performed awesome juggles in that small floating world for us not to have found out about the other until that morning. Jerry's rigid schedule may have helped: she could clock him. I think, though, that Ann managed us—and, we'd suspect later, perhaps one or two junior officers as well—by mostly staying in her cabin between meals and seeing us only briefly in out-of-the-way spots, by appointment. Those Italian Texans!

We were then the only passengers left. Jerry and I had had a great trip, our mother a very quiet one. She hadn't seemed to mind and, anyhow, wouldn't have said if she did. Friendly with all, she'd avoided the cocktail-lounge parties, and spent the time reading, staring in her way, and marching deck laps. So it was nice, in the last few days, to see her suddenly as the centre of officer attention. They vied to walk with her, sit with her, bring her cups of tea and coffee. She glowed a little as on the *Devonshire*.

I visited Sparks more often, even though the list of matters needing to be told was shrinking. We had more easy silences.

Had he read *Forever Amber*?

No.

I'd just finished it.

Well! And?

So-so.

We'd talked about reading before and he'd mentioned books on his shelves, but I hadn't reacted. To suggest outright that I read one was of course not his way.

Forever Amber was so-so, but had I enjoyed the *reading*?

Not much. The trouble was I was always so busy: I didn't have time.

He understood that, but, well, for him, reading was an addiction. He couldn't help himself: he had to read.

Like Jerry and my mother.

Once "ripe" though, Sparks cautioned with a far smile, I'd find it was catching.

He liked evenings to himself, but the night before docking I came up anyway, to say goodbye: there might not be time in the morning. Looming in his doorway, Sparks firmly told me what to do for the second time. Keep my life simple, always simple. Shaking my hand, he said he was sure we'd meet again. People like us always drifted into each other. But that angel-man was wrong about that. We never did.

Just after dawn, my mother was still in her cabin packing, Jerry on the bridge calmly steering us into port. A tugboat puffed alongside far below; it would be delivering the pilot. The tug's rear deck wasn't quite even with our gangplank yet when a nervy boy in short pants leaped across. No, not a boy, a man, a man in a hurry, running up the steps, khaki shirt already blotched with sweat. My God, it was my father!

Dad! Dad! I yelled.

He stopped, looked up, waved, smiled—hey! he looked *glad* to see me! And what a jump he'd made! I ran down to meet him.

He hadn't changed, hair neatly flat, sleeves up in tight rolls. *Jongetje, jongetje,* he said, his voice soft, gripping my hand, blue-grey eyes drilling. My God you've grown!

Still his damn *jongetje* though! I turned from the eyes and pulled him along to my mother's cabin. Startled, she looked unready, hesitant. I left them kissing, and took off to find Jerry.

Then all four of us were in the cabin—Jerry so pleased—and our father told us that, too impatient for the slow docking, he'd hitched a ride with the pilot. Just *had* to see us three! Couldn't wait! Restless and immediately in charge, he worked to shut the bulging suitcase on our mother's bunk, Jerry eagerly helping, and at once spotted my brother's nicotine-stained fingers. The two had a hundred-guilder deal, from when he was fifteen, if Jerry didn't smoke until he was twenty-one. The night before he'd uselessly scrubbed at the yellow with lemon juice.

Our father only murmured, Pity, but the no-nonsense seaman cringed: he'd disappointed already.

Let's go! Let's go! our father urged us, to the lounge to tell the Chief Steward he'd earlier cleared us with customs—paperwork to follow. The moment the *Rondo* tied up, we Hillens could just march off—luggage to follow. He showed us a red card with his picture—Government Information Service: authority. He paced the lounge, hands in pockets, a government man come to fetch his family. Watching him, Jerry's eyes glowed again; our mother's were very alert. And sure, the moment the ship lay still, the Hillens tripped down the gangway, waving at shouting sailors up above—no Sparks. The office Jeep was parked right there waiting.

On the windless wharf, Java's swampy coastal heat hugged us and wouldn't let go. Sweat burst from skin and slicked down. For a moment the steaming air hindered breathing, seeing, even balance. A blink of blackness. Had I, Jesus! *ever been away?* The harbour's oil-shit smell meshed with the heat and said no, kid, you haven't. A *lie*. I *had*. I'd travelled on planes and ships and trains. I'd seen snow, goddammit! and thousands of faces, and thousands of miles of water and land, and leering gargoyles, *baskets* of tomatoes, men and women dancing, windows piled with fruit, a mountain of manure, a snapping turtle. I'd touched bare breasts, heard Niagara Falls and Grand Central Station roaring, smelled schools, tasted rum. . . .

Turning smoothly, our father raced the canvas-topped Jeep down the wharf onto the crowded Batavia road strewn with potholes, which ran for a time beside a scummy canal. From cool unhurried ship time, we had, from the moment our excited father boarded, plunged into a flurry of action. And there we were, short-winded in the Jeep, an hour's drive ahead. And there it was, the land, like bloody yesterday, the rotting patches of deep black greens, shadowless coconut trees, battered bamboo huts, Japanese sun, red dust, and the hellishly shimmering air. I looked down at my feet, at the floor of the Jeep. Jesus! I didn't want to be here! Anywhere but here! I was angry. My wet hands were fists. Then I remembered a nice cooling diary entry, "Think good!" Well, okay . . . What a driver, my father! Fast, sure, and with the reflexes of a fly in that wild blaring traffic. I was impressed. I hadn't known that about him. And there was his jump, too.

We had to yell over the open Jeep's noisy jolting.

No chauffeur! shouted our father. He loved driving himself!

Bully for you! I thought, unkind again.

I was facing the back of his shirt and it was soaked. He leaned towards our mother and said something low—English no more their secret language—and she nodded, and smiled.

Going home, boys! Going home! We are a family!

Old words, I thought.

Sitting behind our mother on the canal side, Jerry's face creased into a wonderful grin. God, the SOB looked happy! His eyes let go of our father only now and then.

We'd love the house he'd rented! We'd have to help build beds though!

Swell. No beds!

Jerry grinned again. Our mother looked over her shoulder and smiled at us. Two years ago, the pink-clothed table in the hotel dining room had felt like our own family island. The rushing Jeep now was also a little world.

Last week, boys, he'd bought a set of beautiful rattan chairs!

Peachy-keen! Mom might've liked a say.

With *orange* cushions!

Marvy!

There was rabies in the city, boys.

Hurrah! Eleven needles in the stomach if a dog bit you.

Our mother then bent sideways to say something private. It was nice, I had to admit, the two of them sitting like that together.

Christ! A corpse! Jerry yelled, pointing to the canal.

I swung around, but too late. I saw lumps of greenish filth on the canal's crusted surface but nothing that looked human. Jerry kept glancing back. Our mother sat facing forward, staring down at her shoes. What was she thinking?

There'd been a lot of fighting! our father shouted. In Surabaya the bastards had burned a busload of women and children!

We hurtled along not speaking for some minutes.

War! We were back in goddamn war! They'll all want independence, Sparks had said. Corpses in canals, burned women and children. In one of his last letters our father had written that things were quiet. *Oh sure!* What the hell were we doing here? Canada, here I come! No killing and burning in Canada! In Canada you had draped gabardine pants, gentle prank players, poems on fishing. Jerry called out questions, about the Dutch army, about Extremists, about this road. Our father shouted answers. The road was absolutely safe. *Sure it was!* Our mother listened round-eyed.

It had been tough for him here, our father shouted a bit later, tough!

Here we go!

My brother and mother watched him.

We know, Dad! Jerry yelled back.

Our mother patted our father's arm, eyes intent; would they stay that way now? I felt as angry as before; thoughts mean and dark. Snap out of it, stupid, I said to myself. I thought of the diary entry: think good, think good. But it didn't work. And yet, wasn't it just a little bit amazing, this family driving home in a Jeep? C'mon good thoughts! I reached then as deep as I could, to when I'd seen the most light, to when I'd felt finest, and it was so simple, such a simple small mercy, because there I was, painting rowboats in the sun on the shore of Rice Lake—just like that!

Another one! Jerry shouted, pointing.

Again I didn't see it. The four of us sat in silence. Was something missing? Yes, there was. My voice. I hadn't said a word. I'd been listening, looking, and thinking nasty thoughts. Hot and thirsty, and though it was so early in the day still, a little tired, we half dozed. We'd talk when we got to Batavia. I should say something though. They had to have noticed, my family, that I hadn't. All three were good that way: at certain times they could let you be. But what to say? What? And then it floated in so easy from Rice Lake, out of "lucid serenity," as my friend Sparks had called it. A very small thing to say, not to be remembered really, but I was certain it fit. All three would like to hear it after my being so quiet. It might set a tone. I wouldn't always be a boy. One day I'd be on a ship plunging through the cold sea towards Canada again. I tapped my father's sweaty shoulder and he leaned back to listen.

I'm damn glad to be here, Dad! I shouted.

I was right. My mother turned and smiled, I felt a little poke from Jerry, my father stuck up his right-hand thumb.

I was just lucky, Sparks had said.